WHAT SHOULD I DO WHEN...

Biblical and Practical Answers to Today's Tough Questions

BILLIE FRIEL

BROADMAN PRESS
NASHVILLE, TENNESSEE

My second book is dedicated to my
second family
The First Baptist family of
Mount Juliet, Tennessee

EPHESIANS 5:25-27

4260-19
ISBN: 0-8054-6019-5
Dewey Decimal Classification: 248.4
Subject Headings: CHRISTIAN LIFE
Library of Congress Catalog Number: 90-34730
Printed in the United States of America

Unless otherwise noted, all Scripture quotations are taken from the *King James Version* of the Bible.

All Scripture notations marked (RSV) are from the *Revised Standard Version of the Bible*, copyrighted 1946, 1952, © 1971, 1973.

Library of Congress Cataloging-in-Publication Data

Friel, Billie Kessner, 1946-
What should I do when-- / Billie Friel.
p. cm.
ISBN: 0-8054-6019-5
1. Christian life--Baptist authors. 2. Pastoral counseling.
I. Title.
BV4501.2.F7635 1991
248.4'861--dc20

90-34730
CIP

Preface

The most often repeated words to a pastor surely must be: "Pastor, what should I do when . . .?" "Man that is born of woman," Job declared, "is of few days, and full of trouble" (Job 14:1). Usually when trouble comes to God's people, they seek for counsel from a man or woman of God. The pastor or committed layperson must be ready to listen, redemptive in purpose, and resourceful in the Word of God when answering the many questions of life.

This book deals with the twelve most pressing questions posed to me in my quarter-century of ministry.

- A man, offered a promotion that involves often leaving home from his teenage children, asks, "What can I do know God's will?"
- While shopping in a grocery store, I run into a member who has received a frightful report from her doctor. She implores, "What can I do now that I am facing this threat to my health?"
- I drive to the airport with a woman to pick up her husband. On the way home this gracious couple breaks the bad news to me, "Pastor, our teenage daughter is pregnant! What should we do?"

The average church family would be amazed how many times a pastor is asked about suicidal tendencies. What would you tell a dear friend to do who is married to a non-Christian? One of the most heart-wrenching scenes occurs when a godly, well-qualified person asks his pastor, "What should I do? I've lost my job." One of the most involved questions is when a person asks what to do when his/her mate has asked for a divorce. Possibly the most-asked question is: "What should I do when I doubt my salvation?"

We are living in alarming ignorance about being able to apply the Bible to our life questions. We should be able to "give an answer to every man" (1 Pet. 3:15) with meekness and fear. Every Christian should be able to "rightly divide the word of truth" (2 Tim. 2:15). Psychology and education are society's "brick for stone and slime for mortar" (Gen. 11:3). Most people want temporary relief and not permanent results.

An old man used to say, "Shutting your eyes to the danger signal does not clear the tracks." This book contains expository answers to pastoral questions. These questions will alert us to danger signals. My fervent prayer is that these Bible answers will clear the tracks.

Contents

1

What Should I Do When . . . a Crisis Comes?

Cancer has returned to the life of a famous actress. The actress, who four years earlier had a mastectomy, announced that the disease has recurred. It is a localized malignancy involving the lymph nodes at the base of the right side of her neck. I was especially interested at the response of this popular actress to this shocking crisis. She remembers her reaction. "I was absolutely terrified. For three days it threw me back into the old feelings of fear." One night she awakened so full of terror that she didn't know what to do. Going into the den, she pedaled for fifty minutes on a stationary bicycle. Since then, the actress has taken out all her old meditation tapes. "Three times a day I visualize my white blood cells as piranha fish destroying my cancer. It stops you feeling like a victim."

How will *you* face a crisis? Will you use meditation tapes, go to Mexico in search of a wonder drug, hibernate, become bitter, or turn to God?

Second Chronicles 20 should become a foundational chapter for each of us when facing a crisis. We should read, review, and rely on the principles found in this precious chapter of God's Word. This chapter is organized into four areas: case, characteristics, cure, and consequences.

Case of Crisis

Our model in learning how to face a crisis is King Jehoshaphat. Several features about Jehoshaphat's life should be mentioned in order that we might appreciate the context of his crisis:

- Jehoshaphat began to reign at age thirty-five and reigned twenty-five years.

- God used him in a great Old Testament revival.
- He was zealous in smashing the idols of Baal.
- He sent home missionaries—itinerant preachers—to instruct the nation in Jehovah's morality.
- The king reorganized his courts and separated church and state.
- He gave swift and impartial administration of justice.
- Jehoshaphat commanded his judges to be just.
- This king had an honest heart and was a man of reverence toward God. He trusted God with his whole heart. He would be ranked as one of Judah's best kings.
- Jehoshaphat "walked in the first ways of his father David" (2 Chron. 17:3)—a true compliment.

And, yet, trouble came to this noble king: unexpected and formidable. Can it happen—a person, minding his own business and doing his best—and then a crisis comes? Yes! Crises often come when a person is working at one's job, caring for one's family, and even when serving one's Lord through the church. Crises are not respecters of persons: "Man that is born of a woman is of few days, and full of trouble" (Job 14:1).

Do you know the number-one topic Ann Landers has dealt with over the years as one of America's counselors? That number-one topic has not been marriage, sex, or work. Receiving 10,000 letters each week for thirty years, Ann Landers announced that the number-one concern over the years has been fear. If *suicide* is the whisper word of America, then *cancer* must be the priority fear of people. People are terrified of the crises of life: sickness, death, job loss, marriage breakup, or personal failure. Fear dominates us, as Ann Landers's study indicates. Do you remember Job's classic words: "For the thing which I greatly feared is come upon me, and that which I was afraid of is come unto me" (Job 3:25)?

So, crises will strike all of God's children. Although a person may be happy, productive, sincere, and a Christian: "Beloved, think it not strange concerning the fiery trial which is to try you, as though some strange thing happened unto you" (1 Pet. 4:12). The question is not if a crisis will come. The question is: "What will I do when it comes?"

Characteristics of Crisis

While Jehoshaphat was riding the crest of a prosperous reign as the king of Judah, a much-feared enemy suddenly appeared to threaten the safety of the king and his people. Notice Jehoshaphat's reaction in verse 3: "And Jehoshaphat feared, and . . ." Let's finish the sentence with some common characteristics of the way people face crises. How could Jehoshaphat have faced the crisis? Let's fill in the blank of "Jehoshaphat feared, and . . ."

Jehoshaphat Feared and Surrendered

This common reaction could have been the initial response of the king. He could have thought: *Syria has a tremendous army, much larger and more fierce than I have. There is no way I can lead these people to victory. If we surrender willingly, probably our nation will be spared from famine, plague, and slaughter.* The king could have surrendered and allowed the enemy to take over.

A common way people face crises is to give in to their fears. One time I heard a man tell about eating oysters. He said if you run into a bad one, you'd better eat another one right away! Don't give in to your fears! Sometimes in golf you have to tee off right beside some woods. Do you know what the professional golfers advise if you're afraid of slicing into the woods? Get as close to the woods as you can when you line up your drive! Face your fears!

I remind you: "God hath not given us the spirit of fear; but of power, and of love, and of a sound mind" (2 Tim. 1:7). Do not surrender to your fears. God will be with you.

Jehoshaphat Feared and Inwardly Resisted

By this we mean that the king could have refused to face the fear. Although the enemy was real, Jehoshaphat could have carried the fear around in him, refusing to face it.

Do you know what happens when people carry fear on the inside and refuse to deal with it? Many times there are physical illnesses. How many cases of ulcers and migraine headaches are among us because people are afraid of something and will not face it. Do you know the only way to destroy an enemy? Make him your friend! We cannot inwardly resist the fear, hoping it will go away. Men are probably more likely to ignore physical warnings than women, aren't they? A man has a pain, and he will try to live with it or cure it himself before going to a doctor. As a result, the illness could worsen bringing serious effects.

Jehoshaphat could have tried to ignore his fear by denying its existence. I remind you: "The Lord is my light and my salvation; whom shall I fear? the Lord is the strength of my life; of whom shall I be afraid?" (Ps. 27:1).

Jehoshaphat Feared and Made a Hasty Alliance

The king could have been motivated by his fear to ask Egypt or some other pagan nation to join him in his fight against the Syrians. This was done frequently and by other kings of Israel and Judah. Because Judah was not strong enough in numbers and armaments, Jehoshaphat could have made an alliance with other nations to strengthen his forces.

Have you ever entered into a hasty alliance because of fear? Have you ever had someone cosign a note for you? Have you ever entered into a business agreement with an ungodly man just to make a hasty financial arrangement? Fear can make us enter into rash covenants which God cannot bless.

Jehoshaphat could have forsaken his trust in the Lord by making an ungodly alliance. I remind you: "But let all those that put their trust in thee rejoice: let them ever shout for joy, because *thou defendest them*" (Ps. 5:11, author's italics). Do not be rash in making decisions! Guidance will be given to you in every crisis. We should submit to God and depend on His timing and method.

Jehoshaphat Feared and Attempted to Cover the Fears

Some adopt this method of facing troubles and crises. Primarily, covering one's fears refers to outside stimulants. A motive behind some drinking and drug use is that of covering one's fears. We have heard the phrase, "Drowning one's sorrows." The problem is, fears do not sink, they float!

Jehoshaphat could have boarded himself up in one of his private rooms and could have drunk himself into oblivion. I know a man who hasn't paid income tax for almost ten years. He also has an alcohol problem, although he puts on a front before the world.

Instead of facing his fears and using his faith, he diminishes his faith and tries to cover the situation with a drink. No, even if Jehoshaphat had resorted to this way of dealing with his crisis, the Syrians still would have been there.

Cure of Crisis

Every need is purposed for personal, spiritual growth and fellowship with our God. Satan will want us to fellowship with some other source and try some other way. Man's extremity does become God's opportunity. Let's answer the question, "What should I do when a crisis comes?" with Jehoshaphat's correct response. What is the biblical way to face a crisis? The answers for Jehoshaphat become our answers, and they come directly from 2 Chronicles 20.

Preparation

Notice verse 3: "And Jehoshaphat feared, and *set himself to seek the Lord*" (author's italics). First of all, there was a spiritual preparation of the heart and soul. To *seek* means to search, try to reach, inquire for, and come to. Jehoshaphat began to prepare himself spiritually to face this crisis. James 4:8 says: "Draw nigh to God, and he will draw nigh to you." We remember the disciples in Jerusalem at Pentecost: They tarried and prayed in seeking the Lord (Acts 1 and 2).

It doesn't matter what the problem is, when someone comes to see *me* as a counselor, invariably I will point them to Proverbs 16:7: "When a man's ways please the Lord, he maketh even his enemies to be at peace with him." Isn't this good advice for Jehoshaphat? Your first priority is to get your heart right with God! Get your heart in the spiritual position where you can hear God and do His will when He reveals it to you.

Have you ever been squirrel hunting? You just don't dash out into the woods and find the game! No, you must become one with the woods. You must be quiet until the woods accept you and go on like normal even though you are there. You must be quiet so you can hear all the sounds. The first step in facing a crisis is to gear down—prepare your heart—in order to hear your God. It's like tuning a piano—our hearts become out of tune by contact with the world. We have to get back in spiritual tune.

Jehoshaphat had a deadline—a definite crisis. Deadlines are great motivators! He began to prepare his heart through fasting (v. 3). As he brought his body into subjection, there was inward victory over outside temptation. Fasting humbled him and brought him into a spiritual condition to hear God. Prepare your heart to seek the Lord and find His will and way when the crisis comes.

Prayer

The natural response to a crisis certainly is prayer. As children, we naturally cry "Father" when trouble arises. Again, let us follow the prayer of Jehoshaphat in verses 5-12. Note in verse 4 that "Judah gathered themselves together, to *ask help of the Lord*" (author's italics). Jehoshaphat's prayer had several noteworthy points:

First, notice his relationship with God.—In verses 6 and 7, God is the God of Jehoshaphat's *fathers* and He is referred to as Abraham's *Friend.* Jehoshaphat claims these relationships as his own: Father and Friend. "For ye have not received the spirit of bondage again to fear; but ye have received the Spirit of adoption, whereby we cry, Abba, Father" (Rom. 8:15). The king's relationship to God as child and friend removed the fear and gave him great confidence to pray.

Second, note Jehoshaphat's recognition of God.—In verse 6, ". . . rulest not thou over all the kingdoms of the heathen? and in thine hand is there not power and might, so that none is able to withstand thee?" Jehoshaphat is recognizing and acknowledging that God is able to handle his problem. "He's got the whole world in His hands." When we realize God can fill them, we will open our mouths wide in big prayers (Ps. 81:10). Remember the words in Hebrews 11:6, "Without faith it is impossible to please him: for he that cometh to God must believe that he is, and that he is a *rewarder* of them that diligently seek him" (author's italics). Jehoshaphat dared to ask for help because he recognized God could and would reward him. How big is your God?

Third, notice Jehoshaphat's realization.—In verse 12, he takes an honest look at his personal resources: "for we have no might against this great company that cometh against us; neither know we what to do: but our eyes are upon thee." The king admitted he and his people did not have the ability to handle this crisis ("no might"). They further confessed that they did not have the wisdom ("neither know we what to do") to solve the problem. We remember when Daniel was faced with the impossible task of not only interpreting Nebuchadnezzar's dream but also revealing his dream. Daniel said, "The secret which the king has demanded cannot the wise men, the astrologers, the magicians, the soothsayers, shew unto the king; *But there is a God in heaven that revealeth secrets*" (Dan. 2:27-28, author's italics). Daniel is saying that there is not a man alive capable of solving this problem. But, there is a God! When our crisis comes, may we strip ourselves of all self-sufficiency and cast ourselves upon God for help and wisdom. "For without me ye can do nothing" (John 15:5).

Fourth, notice Jehoshaphat's reliance on covenant promises.—The king "reminds" God about His promises to Solomon in verse 9: Solomon was told that, when he stood before this house during affliction and called on God, his prayer would be heard and heeded. Man is helpless all the time: It just takes a crisis to reveal it to him! Jehoshaphat's prayer revealed his knowledge of Scripture and his reliance on covenant promises. He boldly claimed God's Word! "For thou hast magnified thy word above all thy name" (Ps. 138:2). The highest form of prayer is praying the Word back to God. Our faith has the Word of God for its source (Rom. 10:17). Know and memorize the Scriptures! Pray them to God! Claim them as your promises for deliverance, healing, and redemption! Pray Philippians 4:19 and 1 Corinthians 10:13 back to God in your own childlike language.

Partnership

Thus far, the way to face a crisis has been preparation and prayer. Here we emphasize partnership with others. Notice verse 4: "And Judah gathered themselves *together,* to ask help of the Lord" (author's italics). A crisis brings people together, doesn't it? "Two are better than one" (Eccl. 4:9-12). "Where no counsel is, the people fall: but in the multitude of counselors there is safety" (Prov. 11:14). We would do well, when crises come, to have spiritual partners with whom we can fellowship and pray.

We remember the desperate prayer meeting in Daniel 2. All the wise men and counselors of the king were about to be executed. Daniel "went to his house, and made the thing known to Hananiah, Mishael, and Azariah, his companions: that they would desire mercies of the God of heaven concerning this secret" (vv. 17-18). Daniel went to his spiritual partners—friends whom he could trust to pray with him and for him. "If two of you shall agree on earth as touching any thing that they shall ask, it shall be done for them of my Father which is in heaven" (Matt. 18:19).

Do you have intimate, confidential, spiritual friends with whom you may pray during a crisis?

Promise

When we seek the Lord, He will be found (Isa. 55:6). God will relate His will to us, primarily through His Word. As Jehoshaphat and the people prayed, the Spirit of God came upon a man named Jahaziel (v. 14). It is unique that Jehaziel was a musician! (There are all kinds of jests the pastors could make at this point!) Please understand that the Spirit's inspiration upon Jehaziel to give him direction is the same Spirit's inspiration which inspired our Bible (2 Tim. 3:16; 2 Pet. 1:21). God was showing the people His will and way through Jehaziel.

Again, we emphasize the importance of knowing the Scriptures. When we hide the Word in our hearts (Ps. 119:11), we will find it again in times of crisis. "My people are destroyed for lack of knowledge" (Hos. 4:6). "Ye do err, not knowing the scriptures, nor the power of God" (Matt. 22:29). God will give us guidance and confirmation through His Word.

Do you remember the time the disciples had fished all night? They had caught nothing and were tired. Jesus gave Simon Peter a command to "Launch out into the deep, and let down your nets for a draught" (Luke 5:4). You remember Peter's response: "Master, we have toiled all the night, and have taken nothing: *nevertheless at thy word* I will let down the net" (Luke 5:5, author's italics). It was not an easy thing to put that heavy net back out! But, Peter trusted his Lord's word and obeyed. You remember the great joy after that. Listen! Quit trying to do it your way and follow the directions! Search the Bible during crisis—God will speak to you! Claim His promise.

Procedure

Do you remember the word of the Lord through Jehaziel? They were told to not fear or be dismayed. They were told to go down against the Syrians and not prepare to fight. God's people were told to set themselves and "see the salvation of the Lord" (vv. 14-17). I'm sure these instructions clashed with the military wisdom of Jehoshaphat's generals!

What have we seen so far in facing the crisis? Preparation of heart, prayer, partnership, promise from God—now, we must proceed and obey God as we've heard Him. Jehoshaphat inspired his people as they began: "O Judah, and ye inhabitants of Jerusalem; Believe in the Lord your God, so shall ye be established; believe his prophets, so shall ye prosper" (v. 20). May I give you a definition of *believe*? Follow His Word. Faith is more than a noun; it is an action verb! People across our country read and know the Bible—the problem is, they do not act on the knowledge they have of the Bible. "But be ye *doers* of the word, and not hearers only, deceiving your own selves" (Jas. 1:22, author's italics). After we know what God is telling us to do, let us begin to do it!

Noah received his instructions and began to build an ark. Abraham received his word from God, packed his bags, and headed out to God's country. Read the roll call of faith in Hebrews 11: Faith is doing! A great verse for this is Hebrews 10:36,"For ye have need of patience, that, after ye have done the will of God, ye might receive the promise." We will not receive the promise until *after* we have *done* the will of God!

So, after you've *prepared* your heart, *prayed*, found *partners*, and claimed your *promise* from God, *proceed* to do His will as you perceive it!

Consequences of Crisis

The victory could not be explained. The people of God started to face the most fierce nation in the world with music, praise, and worship as their weapons! (vv. 21-22). I'm sure the generals were at the *end* of the line covering their eyes! Here they go into battle with the "joy of the Lord" being their strength (Neh. 8:10).

Have you read the end of the story? As His people rejoiced and worshiped, "the Lord set ambushments against the children of Ammon, Moab, and mount Seir" (v. 22). The enemy literally destroyed himself! Unbelievable! Our God "is able to do exceeding abundantly above all that we ask or think, according to the power that worketh in us" (Eph. 3:20). Jehoshaphat and his people had prayed and had received God's answer: "Call unto me, and I will answer thee, and shew thee great and mighty things, which thou *knowest not*" (Jer. 33:3, author's italics).

God has a thousand ways to answer your prayer and meet your crisis. He may use the forces of nature. He may use the instrumentality of other people. He may set "ambushments" for the enemy. God has many ways in which to deliver us from our crisis. Your main need is to *prepare* your heart, *pray,* seek *partners,* claim the *promise,* and *proceed* by doing His will as you perceive it. Let God do the rest!

Oh, yes, one other reminder: Don't forget to give thanks. Read about the return of God's people in verses 27-29. "Psalteries and harps and trumpets"—they returned with joy! A woman called to tell us about the condition of her loved one following a serious surgery. We were so relieved to hear about the success. The woman repeated "Be thankful, be thankful." When God meets your need in your crisis, don't forget to be thankful!

2

What Should I Do When . . . I Am Tempted to Commit Suicide?

Suicide is the taboo subject of America, the "whisper word" of the English language. A pastor is shocked when one of his congregation attempts suicide. A family is devastated when one of their own takes his or her life. Is this a necessary subject? The statistics will answer clearly to the far-reaching effects upon our society. Mental health experts believe that everyone thinks about killing himself at one time or another. Suicide thoughts occur at various levels and stages of people's lives.

Laura was separated from her husband. She had talked to her pastor and Sunday School friends about her situation for several months. No one thought she would commit suicide. One day she came home early, stuffed the air cracks of the garage, and left the car running while sitting in the front seat. When her husband arrived home an hour later, a heavy cloud of black smoke emerged when he opened the garage door. The police chief told me Laura was found dead with her Bible on the seat opened to John 11:25-26.

A famous university in the South was in shock after a rash of suicides. The school was disturbed and mystified after several outstanding students took their lives. The application of suicide seemed almost contagious.

A Nashville funeral home reported that in one year there were over thirty services held where suicide was the cause. In my small town of Mount Juliet, Tennessee, (population less than 4,000), in one year we had four successive funeral services for people who had committed suicide. As far as we could determine, none of the families or incidents were related in any way.

Many believe suicide to be the "unpardonable sin." Many Christians have had relatives to take their lives and wonder if this tendency has been inherited by them. What does the Bible say about death, life, and suicide? We will examine the characteristics, cases, causes, and cure for suicide.

Characteristics of Suicide

- Today, there are an estimated two million people who have tried to take their own lives.
- Fifty thousand people commit suicide each year. These leave an average of five survivors. These people make up a special interest group in our country of 250,000.
- Someone tries to self-destruct every minute of the day.
- Suicide attempts outnumber the deaths eight to one.
- Suicide peak months are from December to May.
- Five thousand youth commit suicide each year. Fifty thousand youth attempt suicide each year. The rate among youth has risen over 250 percent in the last five years.
- Men are 70 percent successful. Shooting or jumping are the ways men choose to take their lives.
- Women are 30 percent successful. They attempt three times more than men. Women usually do not use violent methods that would disfigure the body. Drugs, pills, poison, and carbon monoxide are methods used most often by women.

What kind of person is most prone to self-destruct?

- City people are far more likely than rural people.
- Professional and businessmen are more likely than laborers.
- Single, divorced, and widowed people are more likely to commit suicide than married people. Divorced people under sixty-five are three to five times more likely. Divorced people over sixty-five are two to three times more likely.
- Doctors and lawyers have a rate that is three times higher than other professionals.
- Psychiatrists commit suicide four times more than the general public.
- White people are more likely than black people.
- Vietnam veterans are 65 percent more likely to commit suicide than nonveterans.

• Protestants are more likely than Catholics in the area of suicide. Jewish people are the least likely of all religious groups to commit suicide.

• Letters are left 25 percent of the time. These are often detailed and helpful: They tell how to handle bills and other matters in advance.

• The highest suicide risk is a white male, forty-five years old or older, who is divorced or single.

There are some national differences worth noting. Some feel a life is one's own to give up or keep as one pleases. The Japanese use suicide as a way of avoiding disgrace: hari-kari. Most Christians view suicide as a sin. Many feel that, since one cannot repent of this act, one cannot be forgiven and thus gives up one's hopes of going to heaven. Some believe suicide is a "summons to heaven" and believe it to be one of God's ways to call people home. In many states suicide is against the law, and one is punished for attempting to take one's life.

Cases of Suicide in the Bible

There are six cases of suicide reported in God's Word. We will list and comment on these briefly:

Samson (Judg. 16:29-30)

In thinking about Samson, we always think of "waste." What a man! God used him to deal with the Philistines and bring security to Israel. Samson had two great problems: an uncontrollable temper and uncontrollable passion. He married an unbeliever who betrayed him. Disobedience to God plagued Samson's life repeatedly. Finally, he was captured by his enemies, blinded, and used as a sport. His suicide came as he fantasized a situation in which he could say: "I'll enjoy your suffering even though I have to kill myself."

Saul and Armor Bearer (1 Sam. 31:4-5)

A psychiatrist could have a heyday examining the life of King Saul. He began life with great potential but grievously sinned as power went to his head. This man said, "I'm sorry" more than anyone else in the Bible, but never meant it! Saul dabbled in the occult and witchcraft which opened the way for Satan in his life. At the time of his suicide. Saul had been wounded and was in great physical pain. He had lost hope and knew he had lost favor with God. The king could not bear to be tortured, mocked, and taunted by his enemies. His armor-bearer saw the hopeless situation, also, and followed his king by falling on his sword.

Ahithophel (2 Sam. 17:23)

This man was David's good friend and counselor for many years. When Absalom revolted, Ahithophel switched to the side of the king's son and began to use his counsel against David. It was Ahithophel who gave Absalom the perverted counsel to sleep with his father's wives in front of Israel. At the end of his life, however, Ahithophel's counsel is rejected by Absalom. Feeling disgraced, Ahithophel simply gave up after being fired by Absalom. Bearing a wounded pride, this one-time great counselor lost all hope and turned his aggression toward himself in suicide.

Zimri (1 Kings 16:18)

This man lived a short, violent life! He killed Elah, the king, and massacred the entire seed of Baasha. Then he became king for seven days (the shortest reign of any king) until the city was taken by enemies. The loss of his kingdom overwhelmed him, and he burned the house over himself and died.

Judas (Matt. 27:5)

This is by far the most famous of the biblical accounts of suicide. Judas, at the time of his death, was under great emotional stress. Feeling the enormous guilt of Jesus' betrayal, Judas could not face family, friends, disciples, or even his enemies. Judas depended on Jesus when the two walked together. When Jesus was taken, all emotional support collapsed. His suicide came by hanging. Judas was totally alone during his last moments on earth.

Each of the biblical accounts has a story within itself. We will see as we examine the causes of suicide that many modern-day explanations for suicide were found in the biblical accounts. The Bible is as fresh and up-to-date as tomorrow's newspaper.

Causes of Suicide

While each case is unique, there are eleven causes which have repeatedly been given as reasons for suicide. Examine the list carefully: These symptoms may be seen in situations around us where we live, work, and worship.

Sustaining Serious Loss

Many times we see suicide after a loss of a significant relationship—a mate, relative, or job. There is a devoted attachment to a loved one and, when detachment comes, the bereaved are unable to cope with the events. The lost object is such a part of one's life that continued existence seems unbearable.

Reunion

After a death, relatives (children, youth, or adults) want to rejoin the departed loved one. They feel they will be with them again in heaven.

Loss of Perspective

Many times events loom so large that everything else is obscured. This resembles looking at troubles from the opposite end of the telescope. All that can be seen are the troubles! The universe is narrowed down to one very small blot on which is the word *suicide*. People who self-destruct do not see their total universe: their hopes, family, friends, and future opportunities. To them, their problems are more than they can bear.

Revenge

This cause may be seen in notes left behind. A person fantasizes how he will enjoy the sufferings of the survivors. Satan wrecks their minds so that they want to bring guilt and sorrow to the survivors. A former husband of one of our members called his wife. During the conversation, he said, "There's something I want you to hear." There was a gunshot. He had taken his life and left her with sorrow and guilt.

Guilt-Ridden

Sometimes people take their lives when they feel they deserve punishment for misdeeds. Like Lady Macbeth, they are eaten alive by guilt. In essence, they are trying to wipe away the stain their sins have left. Lady Macbeth cried, "All the perfumes of Arabia will not cleanse this little hand!" A person's unforgiven sins often cause him/her to flaggelate himself—and sometimes even to carry out his/her own death penalty administered by himself. Many a prisoner, even though not sentenced to death, has virtually begged for the death penalty. This is not at all uncommon.

Gain Sympathy

A person is dissatisfied with life. He has experienced feelings of rejection and unworthiness. He wants to shock his friends. This is a very prominent cause.

Humanistic View of Human Life

Today's value system strips people of their dignity and potential. A person is degraded to an animal as he or she is told that this life is all there is—there is no God, heaven, hell, or judgment. People do not realize they was created in the image of God. Without salvation's ennobling influence on people, lives become cheap, without hope.

Unsaved

Those without Christ do not have proper perspectives of life. Their existence has no meaning or purpose. They feel that no one cares for them. A man left a note behind which said: "Life is the process that produces corpses."

Stress

Pressures are upon people today! The job pressures upon a people are tremendous: People must produce and meet critical deadlines each week. A person's self-esteem revolves around one's job, and, if one doesn't succeed, he or she is considered a failure. There can be stresses from one's family life, also, to compound the pressure on one's mind and heart.

Stress forces many professionals to the edge. Rapid technological advances may make one's skills outmoded if one does not practice continuous self-development. This necessitates bringing work home which decreases recreation, outside activities, and family enjoyment. In desperation, the professional reacts with sleeplessness, discord with job and family, absenteeism, ulcers, and, possibly alcoholism. This could lead to thoughts of suicide. This can also apply to ministers!

Loneliness

The bored housewife is a high risk for suicide. This applies to the terminally-ill patient who sees himself as a burden on others. The senior adult ranks at the bottom in threats about committing suicide but ranks at the top of the percentage of completions. The senior adult feels out of place, unproductive, and lonely. Degenerative disease sets in, and hearing and vision are affected. Ill health and financial insecurity compound the issues. When the senior adult tries suicide, he is the most serious and usually succeeds.

Satan

How can we rule out our dreaded enemy? I believe the enemy was behind Job's wife's words: "Curse God, and die" (Job 2:9). I believe Satan whispered into the ear of the Philippian jailer after the earthquake: "Your prisoners are gone. You will be disgraced in front of your family. End life now honorably." Thank God, Paul intercepted him and won him to the Lord! We remember that it was Satan who said to Jesus: "If thou be the Son of God, *cast thyself down*" (Matt. 4:6, author's italics). Satan is a murderer (John 8:44) and is a devouring lion (1 Pet. 5:8). We know that he entered Judas to do that foul deed (Luke 22:3). We remember Satan caused the hogs in Mark 5:13 to commit "hogicide" by drowning in the sea. Who knows the many times Satan has put damning suggestions into people's minds concerning suicide?

While this list is not exhaustive, if you have ever been around an incident of suicide, you will recognize some of these causes being present.

Cure for Suicide

"What should I do when I am tempted to commit suicide?" Satan has the power to interfere with our thoughts about life and, unless we bring into "captivity every thought to the obedience of Christ," the temptation may cross our mind.

May we note at the outset in describing the cure for suicide that it is *not God's will* that we ever take our life! God is the giver of life, and only He has the power to take it away. If ever the temptation or thought comes across your mind, recognize the source of that thought—the devil!

A discussion of a key verse may be helpful at this point. Jesus spoke helpful words for us in John 10:10: "The thief cometh not, but for to steal, and to kill, and to destroy: I am come that they might have life, and that they might have it more abundantly."

Notice the *two masters.* Satan is represented by the "thief" in this passage. Jesus Christ is represented by the "shepherd." Both are real persons with recognizable characteristics.

Notice the *two missions* of the two masters. Satan's mission is to "steal, and to kill, and to destroy." If he could, Satan would steal our happiness and destroy our lives. The devil is a liar and a murderer (John 8:44). He is an agent of destruction, and one of his weapons is suicide. However, notice the mission of Jesus, "I am come that they might have *life*" (author's italics). Jesus is the great Life Giver. At salvation we are born from above and receive life from God. There are two main words for life in the New Testament: *zoe* and *bios*. (Zoology and biology come from these two words). *Zoe* is intensive, while *bios* is extensive. *Zoe* (used here in John 10:10 and 3:15) is the nobler word and expresses all of the best and highest which the child of God possesses in God.

God's desire is that we have *zoe,* life from Him that is eternal and "abundant." The word for *abundant, perissos,* has a mathematical meaning and generally denotes a surplus. God tells us that, not only will He give quantity of life that is eternal, but also quality of life that is abundant. God's life in us gives us a noble purpose for which to live. There is a surplus of blessings that can cancel any temptation to end one's life by suicide.

So, with life eternal and life abundant in us, suicide can be forever erased from the Christian's vocabulary. However, let's briefly name several practical suggestions answering the question, "What should I do when I am tempted to commit suicide?"

Get Off Pills and Drugs

How Satan uses hallucinatory elements in our culture today! Drugs have satanic kickbacks that are deadly and have caused people to jump out windows thinking they could fly! Let God be the Source of your peace and strength. "Thou wilt keep him in perfect peace, whose mind is stayed on thee" (Isa. 26:3).

Handle Rejection in a Spiritual Way

Realize that opposition and losses will come. Failure is not the end of the world. We must learn from our mistakes and keep going. "If we confess our sins, he is faithful and just to forgive us our sins, and to cleanse us from all unrighteousness" (1 John 1:9). You can do "all things" through Christ (Phil. 4:13).

Build Your Life Around God

Idolatry can be the overemphasis of people and things! Therefore, when detachments or separations come, the person is unable to cope with the loss. Put God first in your life: "But seek ye first the kingdom of God, and his righteousness; and *all these things shall be added* unto you" (Matt. 6:33, author's italics). Joy is still true—Jesus, others, you.

Set Realistic, Godly Goals

What does God want to accomplish with your life? Remember that a human's life "consisteth not in the abundance of the things which he possesseth" (Luke 12:15). We should learn to have contentment in life (1 Tim. 6:6-8). The "love of money" is still the root of all evil, and many have been pierced with sorrow because their main goal was the acquisition of material wealth. Let your main goals be doing everything to the glory of God (1 Cor. 10:31) and making your ways pleasing to Him (Prov. 16:7). Pray about and set realistic, godly goals.

Straighten Out Your Home

With all the pressures on a person in the world, where does one turn if he or she doesn't have a godly home or Bible-believing church? Love, compassion, and acceptance from a happy home have prevented many suicides. "United we stand, divided we fall." Christ must be Savior and Lord of our homes. "Except the Lord build the house, they labour in vain that build it" (Ps. 127:1). If all are saved in the home and troubles come, pray, search the Scriptures, confess to one another, open the lines of communication, and seek counsel from godly friends or leaders (Prov. 11:14).

Be Satisfied with Aging

Do not let Satan discourage you as you grow older. The best is always yet to be. Be faithful. Remain active and ready to serve (remember Caleb). Keep your body in subjection (1 Cor. 9:27). Recycle your mind by seeking God in His Word (Rom. 12:2; Ps. 1:2). Someone has said that Satan never has any happy elderly men—is that true? May God invigorate and bless your senior adult life the way He did for Moses (Deut. 34:7).

Be Involved with People

The majority of suicides come as people become lonely and isolated. Remember how discouraged Elijah and John the Baptist became when separated from people. Do not wallow in loneliness! Attend the services and fellowships! Invest in the lives of others. I believe my mother would have been dead several years ago if she had not had the fellowship of godly women in her church.

Remember God's Love for You

People who self-destruct develop the mind-set that no one cares for them. At the time of suicide, one's self-worth is at an all-time low. Please remember that our true sense of self-worth is not based on society's standards or what people think about us! Our position in Christ gives us our true sense of self-worth. Let us organize our personality around the security God provides. Like the psalmist, we can say: "When my father and my mother forsake me, then the Lord will take me up" (Ps. 27:10).

Know that God Is in Charge

Have you read the last chapter in the Book? All needs are happily ever after! Realize that an all-knowing, all-powerful God is in charge of your life and you can trust Him. A father and his little girl were going up the elevator of the Empire State Building. Up, up, they went until the little girl said, "Daddy, does God know we're coming?" Yes, God is in charge, and He knows you're coming! Sometimes we have tunnel vision when we look at circumstances through a long, dark tunnel. We see only darkness and do not realize there is light at the other end. We think the darkness will go on forever. Do know God will work things out for good (Rom. 8:28).

Be Sensitive to People's Cries for Help

Experts feel 80 percent of the suicides could have been averted. There will be visible symptoms in many cases: depression, withdrawal, giving things away, talking about wills, sleeplessness, too much sleep, or people may mention suicide directly or indirectly. Stressful situations lead to frustration, despair, and depression. Some time events are viewed as unbearable, and death is seen as a merciful release from the pain of life. Eventually, the person sees suicide as the common sense resolution to an unchangeable reality. Watch over people (Heb. 3:13). We are our brother's keeper!

Don't Ever Entertain Thoughts of Suicide

Know that the devil is the initiator of such thoughts. Satan will always make things bigger than they are. He will try to convince us that no one cares, especially God. The enemy will attempt to overload people with so much guilt that suicide is considered (2 Cor. 2:7,11).

The mother of a wonderful family lay very sick. Tenderly she told her family she was dying. "I've shown you for thirty-five years how a Christian ought to live. Now I'm going to show you how to die." Dying grace will come when we need it. Until then, let us live our lives unto the Lord and cherish His abundant life!

3

What Should I Do When . . . I Grow Old?

The clock is ticking. Time is passing. Each of us is growing older every single minute. Aging is not a popular thought in this land of youth and honey. We realize this when multiplied millions of dollars are spent each year in cosmetics, diet aids, hair dyes, and exercise programs in a desperate attempt to roll back the years and avoid the inevitable.

Our generation has been called the "Pepsi Generation," but there is a switch to Geritol that is happening! We are witnessing what has been called the "Graying of America." This is evident from the following facts:

- Sixteen percent of our population is sixty and over.
- People over seventy form the fastest growing segment of society. As a matter of fact, this segment is growing twice as fast as any other part.
- Our nation has over 32,000 people who are 100 years of age or older!
- The average person's life span in America today is seventy-four.

Women can expect to live to seventy-eight, and men can expect to live to seventy. This is phenomenal when one considers that in 1900 the average life span was only forty-seven. The human life span is twice as long as the chimpanzee's and sixty times longer than a mouse. Only the giant tortoise, the world's longest-living creature at 152 or more, lives longer.

There are three great facts we must admit as we study what God's Word says about aging. First, aging is universal: Everyone will grow older. Second, aging is progressive. We go through the stages of infancy, childhood, youth, adulthood, and older adulthood. No one skips a stage, and each person passes through these stages at his or her own pace. Third, aging is irreversible. That is, we cannot turn back the clock. There is no repeating of a stage in our life.

Once there was an old man who wanted to be young again. He went to see the doctor and asked, "Doc, do you have any pills that would make me young again?"

The doctor replied, "Yes, I do. These are the most powerful pills known to man. Take one a day for six days and come see me."

The old man happily drove home and pondered as he drove, *Why wait? Why not take all six tonight and become young in one night?* So, before retiring that night, the old man took all six pills. The next morning his wife awakened and felt where he usually slept. He wasn't there. She looked all around the house for him but could not find him.

Finally, she looked outside and, there he was, sitting on the steps, crying. She stuck her head out the door and inquired, "Honey, what's wrong?"

The old man replied to her in a childlike voice, "I mithed my buth!"

We must remember that aging is universal, progressive, and irreversible. As a matter of fact, there are two ways in which we age. One is chronologically. This is where we have a definite calendar age which is absolute and cannot be changed. The other way in which we age, however, is physiologically. In this aspect of aging, one's physical progress may vary tremendously from one's chronological age. It also varies vividly from person to person. In some people the chronological age and the physiological seemingly never come together.

What should I do when I grow old? What an interesting, important subject! It appears that our country is more "senior-adult conscious" than ever before. Movies such as *Cocoon* and *Amos* have brought the needs of the aged to our attention. The television series "Golden Girls" is at the top of the chart in popularity. But, what does the Bible say about aging? Let's look at this subject in the following aspects: characteristics, changes, cases, and cure for growing old.

Characteristics of Aging

All of us are aware of the fact that we are not the same person we were when we were younger. Time has a way of producing changes in us. What are these characteristics of growing old? The following information can be most revealing and may disturb some of you! Brace yourself! Let's examine the physiological and psychological characteristics of aging.

Physiological Characteristics

The most vivid proof of aging is physical features. Come with me as we examine the effects of aging upon our body.

Hair.—Probably the first evidence of aging is that of the hair. It may surprise you to know that men do grow hairier with age, but not where it does them good! Some men's hair turns gray while others' turn loose! Hair continues to grow in the ears, nose, and on the back, but due to different hormones at work, the head is diversely affected. Balding begins at the temples with men and moves at different rates. The hairs thin with age until by seventy one's hairs are as fine as when he was a baby. Also, just like a plant losing the supply of chlorophyll which causes fading, the hair's supply of nutrients is gradually cut off until grayness occurs. The marks of the aged's hair is a mark of honor, however, "The hoary head is a crown of glory, if it be found in the way of righteousness" (Prov. 16:31).

Skin.—In some ways we make our own wrinkles. The lines of one's face come from repeated facial expressions. As we age, the inside of the skin loses water, and the skin structure becomes stiff and less elastic. The skin spreads out like dough that is stretched with the result being a baggy suit with the skin too large for the body. Doctors warn us of two great dangers to our skin: the exposure to the sun and smoking. These may make one look ten to twenty years older than one really is.

This pastor was put in his place recently on a mission trip to South Dakota. The Indians are so honest! We had over one hundred Sioux children on a bus going to Vacation Bible School one morning. Each of the leaders had children sitting all over them. I had two beautiful little Indian girls sitting on my lap. For the first half hour they studied me carefully. They looked at my hair and pinched my arms. Finally, one said, "His hair tells us he is old, but his skin is young!" Our hair and skin will give us away!

Eyes.—As we age, the lenses of the eyes steadily harden and begin to cause problems for us in our forties. By then, the lenses are too big for the eye muscles to focus properly on close objects. Cataracts may grow. Also, the amount of light reaching the retina steadily deteriorates with age, and one will have trouble seeing in the darkness. Bright light will be needed for the aged person to read properly.

Hearing.—With aging, the hearing of the sounds on the upper end of the frequency scale is lost. Many people will have a ringing or buzzing sound in their ears due to defects in the inner ear. Ear wax may increase, and professional help is needed. Deteriorating nerve fibers cause one's hearing ability to go from 15,000 hertz, or the sound of a cricket's chirp, to 6,000 hertz, or the sound of the organ's high notes. The average person, as he ages, will continue to be able to hear the 4,000 hertz of everyday human speech.

Height.—People can withstand gravity's pull only so long! As muscles weaken, one's back slumps. With time, disks between the bones of the spine deteriorate, and these bones move closer together. The result is the shrinking person who may lose up to an inch and a half in height as he or she ages.

Taste.—Aging reduces taste. At age thirty, each tiny elevation on the tongue (papilla) has 245 taste buds. At age seventy, these papilla have only eighty-eight taste buds. The mouth gets drier as mucous membranes secrete less. Vocal cords control lessens. The voice quivers, pitch rises, and one's talk becomes slower.

Teeth.—Eating slowly files down our teeth, but most of tooth and gum decay is a result of neglect. The amount of enamel on the surface will decrease while the layer of dentin underneath will become more translucent. The average seventy-year-old has lost about one-third of his teeth.

Bones and joints.—Life is a constant battle against gravity. Gradually the fight is lost, and the body sags. The blood vessels clog up. The bones lose calcium and become more brittle and slower to heal. Years of flexing wear down and loosen cartilage around the joints. The lubricating fluid in the joints is depleted over the years and makes for slower movement and greater stiffness. Ligaments contract and harden with age, making one more susceptible to ligament tears and injury. Truly, the outward man is perishing day by day (2 Cor. 4:16).

We should note, however, that when gerontologists want to determine the extent to which a person has aged, they don't look for streaks of gray hair or crow's feet around the eyes. They look for "biomarkers of aging." These are: strength of a person's grip, the amount of lung capacity, the size of the pupils, the sleep patterns, strength of the immunity system, the amount of bone loss, and one's reaction time.

Psychological Characteristics

George Burns, the aged comedian, commented recently: "I can't die! I'm booked for years!" The physical characteristics are usually most evident in the aged, but there are also psychological characteristics of aging which we shall note. The main features of psychological aging are as listed.

- Intellectual decline is more related to disease and illness than it is to aging.
- The aged perform lower in experiments demanding immediate and short-term recall. Numerical calculations and speed response seem to diminish with age. Verbal functioning continues to increase throughout one's life span.
- After thirty, a person loses about 1 percent of functional capacity each year. The cells disappear, tissue stiffens, and chemical reactions slow down.
- At age thirty-five, the 10 billion cells of the brain began to die at the rate of 100,000 a day.

Changes of Aging

Aging ushers in vast changes to one's life. These changes are often seen as crises. Three main crises for the aged appear.

Identity Crisis

As one reaches senior adulthood, a person eventually gives up the work role that has been the focus of his daily activity for the major part of his life. Though a person's skills may not have changed dramatically, one is now forced to be cut off from the mainstream of society. In doing this, one takes a drastic cut in income. A person is also now viewed as a dependent.

Statistics show that 79 percent of people nearing sixty-five would prefer to continue in part-time work after retirement. Retirement is dangerous to one's health, if one is suddenly cut off from being productive. This role shift requires the adoption of an entirely new life-style which is often accompanied by the loss of self-esteem.

Activity Crisis

There is also a change in one's physical activity. As one ages, there is a reduced mobility as well as declining physical endurance. This crisis can produce anxiety and embarrassment.

Some statistics prove to be alarming in the activity crisis area.

- Seven million elderly live alone. Eighty percent are women.
- There are over 23,000 nursing homes in America. Five percent of the elderly live there. One in five will enter a nursing home at some point. The average age in nursing homes is eighty. Fifty percent have no family. Fifty percent have some mental disorder.

When one realizes that one-third of all suicides are elderly people, we see the alarming effect of the activity crisis.

Acceptability Crisis

Old is a difficult adjective to describe oneself with. People often reject the fact of bodily changes and may be reluctant to confirm their age status through association with groups of older people. At our church we have a difficult time enlisting people to join our "Elderbloom Ministry." They will not admit their age!

This acceptability crisis prompts us to ask, "When is one considered a senior adult?" Social Security recognizes the age of sixty-two. Company retirement plans normally go with the age sixty-five. Someone has said that we are as old as our teeth but not as old as our hair! Eventually a person has to bow before Father Time and admit he or she has become a senior adult. My grandmother used to say that one is either pickled in vinegar or honey, and we can choose the one we want! It is important that one accepts his or her age and status in society and begins to live that new part of his or her life to the fullest.

Cases of Aging

God is in charge of our lives! He intends for us to become better, not bitter. I used to dread growing old until I met some tremendous senior citizens who were productive and happy in life.

All of us have heard the myths about aging: "You can't teach an old dog new tricks." "There's no fool like an old fool." "His best years are behind him." "Oh, to be young again."

But, listen! God is in charge. He will allow us to live as long as we have purpose, meaning, and productivity in life. My grandfather lived to be ninety-two and what a man! What a mind! What a ministry in life! Look at some of the following great senior adult's lives.

- Moses did his most significant work after eighty years of age.
- Caleb climbed mountains after giants until he was eighty-five.
- Michelangelo painted and sculpted, when he was in his seventies and eighties.
- Benjamin Franklin helped draft the Declaration of Independence at age seventy.
- Connie Mack and Casey Stengel were tremendous baseball managers in their seventies and eighties.
- Grandma Moses had arthritis at seventy-six and began to take up painting, because she could not embroider.
- Amos Alonzo Stagg was a successful football coach in his eighties.
- Pearl Buck wrote a novel at age sixty-seven.
- Karl Menninger, noted psychologist, wrote *Whatever Became of Sin?* at seventy-five.
- Winston Churchill did his most statesman-like work after age sixty-five.
- The work of John Wesley was at its best in his eighties.
- Two of our finest presidents were respected statesmen, when they were ninety (Herbert Hoover) and eighty-eight (Harry Truman).

• Who knows the ages of Bob Hope and Ginger Rogers? These entertainers continue to thrill us year after year. Both play golf and tennis.

Several years ago, I had Dr. Robert G. Lee in my church for a revival. At that time, Dr. Lee was eighty-nine years of age. What a man and mind! He spoke seven times and never opened a book. Our people and my family loved him. He gave all of us the desire to grow old with the Lord.

Satchel Paige, the wily black pitcher, used to comment, "Don't look back. Someone might be gaining on you!" These cases should encourage us to look forward to serving God as long as He allows us to live.

Cure of Aging

Our original question was, "What should I do when I grow old?" Very possibly the answer to that question might be according to the "bed in which you were born!" Heredity and physical environment play such important parts to our aging process. But, God's Word does have some definite principles that will help us grow old productively and gracefully.

A tremendous senior citizen is described in Luke 2:36-38. Her name is Anna. Let us look at several features of her life that will help us to grow old.

Wife

Anna was married at a young age. I believe she followed God's will in the selection of a husband. No doubt Anna and her husband had a happy life together for the seven years of their marriage.

Widow

Most scholars believe the age of marriage for a young girl was about fifteen at that time. If we accept this age for Anna, then she became a widow at age twenty-two. For the next sixty-two years Anna lived alone as a widow. God did not lead her to remarry, and she lived many years joined to Him as her provider and protector. We know that the loss of a mate is one of the greatest crises in one's life and produces unbelievable stress. How was

Anna able to handle this tragedy in her life? Many widows and widowers never make it back into society but stay as recluses and hermits the rest of their lives. One of the founding fathers of Nashville died, and it was spoken of his widow, "She never crossed Broadway again." How was Anna able to handle this tragedy in her life?

Worshiper

Anna handled the tragedy by leaning on God. The Scripture says that she "departed not from the temple, but served God with fastings and prayers night and day" (v. 37). In this passage we see that there were two forms of Anna's worship: private and public. There is no way a person can grow or be sustained without private worship—reading, studying, praying, meditating, and having intimate fellowship with God. "Be still, and know that I am God" (Ps. 46:10). But we also need public worship as we learn, lean, laugh, and listen to our family in the faith. Anna went to the house of God where she sang the songs of faith, heard the Word of God preached and taught, and felt the warmth of family fellowship.

How we can learn from Anna at this point in her life! Some turn to God in crises and others turn away from God. I believe Anna's private devotional life prepared her for the public crisis of widowhood. I also believe that her church was a blessing to her in the time she needed comfort and encouragement.

Worker

Anna also "served" God as a senior adult. She was a "doer of the word, and not a hearer only" (see Jas. 1:22). My own mother has been such an example to me as she has faced senior adult years. Divorced over twenty-five years, my mother has never thrown in the towel: She has continued to grow spiritually and is now closer to God than I've ever known her to be. She speaks in psalms, hymns, and spiritual songs and makes melody in her heart (Eph. 5:19). Also, she now serves in the bus ministry at a small Florida church and is thrilled to fill her bus for the Lord each week. One cannot give up but must keep serving the Lord.

How can we learn from Anna in her working for God as a senior adult? I see so many senior adults turn to shuffleboard, crocheting, playing cards, or fishing in the last years. Why can't we use these years to serve God? God has given the senior adult much valuable time that could be spent in service.

Witness

We note in our Scripture that Anna gave witness to Christ. She had worshiped His Father so many years that she instantly recognized His Son when He was brought into the temple! It is said that she spoke "of him to all them that looked for redemption in Jerusalem" (v. 38). The greatest service we can ever render to our Lord is to be a witness for Him.

I read some statistics that disturbed me. The Harris Poll revealed that 71 percent of people over sixty-five found religion very important to them. But, next to God, what older Americans draw closest to is television! Senior adults have a viewing time that is triple that of the national average. One senior adult said, "Television gives me life. It gives me what to look forward to—that tomorrow, if I live, I'll watch this and that program!" The survey indicated that only 39 percent of elderly people read regularly, as compared to the national average of 56 percent.

Oh, how I desire to be used of God all the way to the end! God, give us senior adults who will tell others of Jesus! There are so many aged ones who are lost, and they have so much potential for the Lord. John Rice Irwin, founder of the Museum of Appalachia in Norris, Tennessee, researched older people in the mountains and collected old items to preserve their heritage. Irwin said, "When an old person dies, it's like a small library burning." May God make us to be fervent witnesses of Him as we grow old!

What should I do when I grow old? It would shock you to learn that you are actually preparing for this by the way you live now each day. You will come into senior adulthood the way you are now, only better or worse. Let me suggest several checkpoints to help you face senior adulthood:

First, what about your *priorities*?—Is God first in your life? Surely you do not have any gods before Him. Read Matthew 6:33 and Proverbs 3:5-6. Check your priorities and make sure Jesus is Lord of all that you are and have.

Second, what about your *prayer life*?—Do you have a daily quiet time each day? Anna was prepared for the public crisis in her life because she had learned to serve God by prayer and fastings. Develop the inward person of the soul. Spend time with God in secret by praying, meditating on the Scripture, and having fellowship with Him.

Thirdly, what about your *physical condition*?—Is your body a fit temple for the Holy Spirit? Many people approach senior adulthood with broken bodies that will not last long after retirement. Eat balanced meals with vegetables, brans, chicken, fish, and water. Develop some form of acceptable exercise that you can continue into senior adulthood.

Fourthly, what about your overall *program of life*?—By this I mean, is your life balanced? There should be prayer, Bible study, fellowship, and witnessing in your life. Many people enter senior adulthood without hobbies, friendships, or plans for retirement. Examine your life, your interests, and your abilities. Develop a program of activity, production, relationships, and fellowship that will continue on into senior adulthood. Have a balanced life.

Finally, what is your *purpose in life*?—What does God want you to do? Plan to stay off the shelf! I do believe that I have seen senior adults die within the first few years of retirement because of loneliness, boredom, and feeling worthless. Retirement can be dangerous according to my experience of watching people over the years. The Scripture says, "Where there is no vision, the people perish" (Prov. 29:18). Could we not apply this to looking forward to growing old? Preparing for aging is like an investment—plan for it! Make good decisions. Choose the godly life-style that will yield good returns and increase in value.

What should I do when I grow old? What a question! Let Anna be our example as we prepare for senior adulthood. God should be first in our lives through our worship, work, and witness.

4

What Should I Do When . . . My Teenage Daughter Becomes Pregnant?

The unique event happened on a Sunday night. My message that morning had come from Galatians 6:1 and had dealt on how the church should treat a person overtaken in a fault. I stated that we had three choices: rock them, reject them, or restore them. Now, in the evening service, a man approached the pulpit and wanted to speak. I trusted the man and stepped away from the pulpit to let him speak.

He spoke humbly: "Folks, my family and I are in trouble. Our teenage daughter is pregnant. As we thought and prayed about this, we had several options. One, we could have an abortion. Two, we could send our daughter to Texas to an aunt where she could live comfortably and have the baby in secret; however, we ruled this out because she needs us now more than she ever has. Three, we could go about our business as usual, have the baby, and face all the gossip and rumors that will come. Or, fourthly, we could come before our church family, confess, and ask for your forgiveness and support."

With that announcement, the bomb was dropped. Before a soul could move, the mother approached the pulpit. She quoted Lamentations 3:22, "It is of the Lord's mercies that we are not consumed, because his compassions fail not." She told us what a shock this was to their family, how rough the final decision was, and asked for our prayers.

As the mother stepped away from the pulpit and merged with the congregation, the pregnant daughter came forward. "I've sinned," she began. "I've sinned against God. I've sinned against my body. I've sinned against my baby. And I've sinned against you, the church. Please forgive me!"

I went back to the pulpit and said, "This morning I preached on how to treat someone overtaken in a fault. The options were that we could rock them, reject them, or restore them. I don't know about you, but I vote to restore them!" With that, I motioned for the family to come back down front, and I gave all of them a big hug. Then, I stepped back to see what would happen next. People began to come forward to hug and encourage that family. It was wonderful and fulfilled Galatians 6:1 perfectly!

"What should I do when my teenage daughter becomes pregnant?" This seems to be a topic of intense conversation today. We've seen it discussed on television, read about it in newspapers and magazines. Teen pregnancy is a problem for the school system, social workers, church, and family.

A major morning television program ran a documentary about teenage pregnancy for an entire week. During that coverage, a high school sophomore was asked to give the number of pregnant friends she had. "I really don't know," she quipped, "but it seems like I am going to more baby showers than social parties!"

Let's divide this topic into the following parts: cases, consequences, causes, and cure for teenage pregnancy.

Cases of Teen Pregnancy

The statistics speak for themselves. Please prayerfully note the following information.

- Of the 21 million teenagers in the United States, it is estimated that 12 million are sexually active.
- There were over 1.1 million pregnancies among teenagers last year.

Six hundred thousand babies were born to teenagers; children are having children at the rate of almost 2,000 a day! That's seventy per hour.

- Ninety percent of these babies will be kept by their mothers.
- Our country has the highest teenage pregnancy rate of any industrial country in the world.
- There are over 30,000 pregnancies to girls under fourteen.
- Forty percent of fourteen-year-old girls will be pregnant at least once before twenty years of age.

- One out of ten teenage girls will become pregnant before they are twenty years of age.

These are the cases. The statistics are awesome. Our hearts break because of the happenings among teenagers today. In my own state of Tennessee, two teens become pregnant every hour. In 1987, fifteen twelve-year-olds were pregnant, and nine became mothers. There were fifty-eight births to thirteen-year-olds from 115 pregnancies. In 1987, there were 2,509 abortions to girls age seventeen and younger.

Consequences of Teen Pregnancy

What are the results of a teenager becoming pregnant?

To the Mother

A girl under sixteen has a greater chance of serious health problems during pregnancy than an older woman. The cases of maternal death is 60 percent higher for pregnant teenagers fifteen years or under than those who are in their twenties. Fifty percent of these girls never have health care during the first trimester during their pregnancy. Some of the complications are hypertension, high blood pressure, toxemia, premature or prolonged labor, abnormal heart rate, anemia, and gestational diabetes.

To the Baby

Many times the teenager has poor eating habits and tends to starve herself. When this happens, her baby is underweight. The mortality rate is double that than for infants born to mothers in their twenties. The infant mortality rate indicates that 6 percent of the babies born to girls fifteen years of age or under die during the first year. Babies of teens have a 30-50 percent higher chance to have a serious birth defect. When this happens, the babies are more likely to be blind or deaf. Studies show children who are underweight, with poor nutrition being the cause, can account for 80 percent of the learning disabilities and 50 percent of the mental retardation. It is estimated that 90 percent of cerebral palsy could be eliminated by proper nutrition before birth.

Economic

Eight out of ten girls who become pregnant as teenagers under seventeen will never finish high school. This puts them at a disadvantage with their job earning potential. Sixty percent of the children born out of wedlock will end up on welfare. Forty percent of the teen mothers will have another baby within a year. Seventy percent will have another child within two years. The financial difficulty will always be there. One-half of the mothers will rear their children as single parents, and this means there will be a continual poverty struggle. If the teen mother finds a job, it would probably be in a restaurant, motel, or retail sales position where the salary is minimum wage with little or no benefits. If the teenage mother marries, the marriage is two to three times more likely to end in divorce than those marrying in their twenties.

Child Abuse

Fifty percent of all child abuse is by teenage mothers. Child abuse is five times more likely to happen by teen mothers than by mothers in their twenties.

Guilt

The above consequences are the visible factors, but what about the invisible consequences? The little girl begins to realize she has violated her body and desecrated the privacy and sanctity of her vessel. She asks for forgiveness, but there will still be a dark cloud over her life. It hurts when the realization comes home of the lost youth during the years of fifteen to twenty. Some times the kickback occurs when a boy blames a girl for tying him down all the years of older teenhood. A girl will look around and suddenly see that she is "old." The suicide rate for pregnant teenagers is seven times higher than for other people. Pregnancy outside of wedlock is a sin that cannot be hidden. Severe consequences follow.

Causes of Teen Pregnancy

What are the causes of teen pregnancy? I believe we should examine them, pray about them, and see what the roles of the church and family are in helping with them.

Ignorance

The world would have us think that ignorance is the main cause of the teen pregnancy epidemic. The unchurched world would have us believe that all we have to do is teach youth about the body and birth control. The secular world would have the teen to know four or five different methods of intercourse and some basic facts about the human body.

But do you hear the subtle advice the world is giving when ignorance is given as the main cause? The secular system teaches that sex out of wedlock is all right—the main fact is to be responsible. I saw this fallacy illustrated on television when a famous expert on sex was interviewed. This expert's main theme was that sex, any kind of sex, is right as long as it takes place between two consenting adults. She concluded that it didn't matter if the two consenting adults were two men together, two women together, or a married man and a single woman together—they merely had to consent!

The Word of God declares that responsible sex for a teen is *abstinence!* Hebrews 13:4 says: "Marriage is honorable in all, and the bed undefiled: but whoremongers and adulterers God will judge." The marriage is to be pure! There is to be no sex before marriage. I do not want my child being told by a school teacher (even a Christian school teacher!) about the proper use of the birth control pill, the parts of the body, or any other facet of sex education. The father and mother should pray with their children and instruct them in the "facts of life." The only responsible sex for a teenager is abstinence.

Denial

Some teenagers become pregnant because, although they have heard the scriptural counsel, they choose to deny it. Many have the kind of heart and spirit where they reject counsel and ignore commands. They will have sex. Statistics show that about half of all teen pregnancies occur in the first six months of sexual activity. "There is a way which seemeth right unto a man, but the end thereof are the ways of death" (Prov. 14:12).

Peer Pressure

Many experts believe pressure from one's peers is the number-one cause of teen pregnancy. Friends of the teenager will say: "What are you waiting for?" "You mean, you haven't done it yet?" "You ought to try it—everybody else is doing it!" Did you know that *no* is the hardest word to say in any language? But Joseph said "no" when he was tempted by Potiphar's wife! He said, "How then can I do this great wickedness, and sin against God?" (Gen. 39:9). Our trouble may be that the youth do not realize premarital sex is "great wickedness against God."

So much pressure is placed on a girl from her boyfriend. The boyfriend says: "If you won't do this, you don't love me." Yet, you know deep down a person who loves someone will not force them to do something that is wrong. Also, a person who loves you will respect your beliefs. One of the things we need to bring out into the open is the confusion between making love and making babies. There is a difference between love, commitment, an undefiled bed, and marriage and a guy saying "I want to give you a baby!" Boys should not say, "I love you" when they are not thinking and feeling true love at all. The principle is: a girl will give sex to obtain love and a boy will give love to gain sex. True love means planning a wedding, counseling with the pastor, a wedding ring, a Christ-like ceremony, and a life-long commitment. "Marriage is honourable in all"; write it down!

Peer pressure has about made virginity a vanishing species. Pastors and counselors estimate today that only one in five girls coming to the marriage bed are virgins. The figure is more shocking for boys. Twenty-five years ago, 50 percent of the women and men who approached marriage were virgins. I always wonder when I perform a marriage if the participants are pure. The priceless gift of virginity has been influenced by the decline of religion, the liberal climate of the time, the introduction of the pill and birth control, and the rising number of women who postpone their marriage for a career.

Poor Relationship with Family

Often a teenager having a baby comes from a broken home, a home where the father is not the example and where the mother is not present. An expert in Nashville with whom I talked suggested that I watch the example of the father. Little girls are affectionate, and they want love and attention from their father. If the father does not give it to them, they will seek that affection somewhere else. The father is also the protector and shepherd. The devil cannot come into the strong man's house and spoil his goods unless he binds the strong man (Matt. 12:29). Satan is having a heyday spoiling the precious goods of our homes because the father is absent or does not have his gospel armor in place (Eph. 6:10-18). Fathers should pray over children, keep up with them, and protect them. Job prayed over his children every day (Job 1:5).

The example of the parents is tremendously important. Let me share with you a stunning statistic: 22 percent of the pregnant teenagers were from mothers who also had been pregnant as teenagers. Like mother, like daughter. I knew of a situation twenty-five years ago where a girl became pregnant while in high school. In those days, that kind of situation was scandalous. However, within two years, she had another baby by the same boy. There was no marriage between the father and mother of the children, but later the girl married a fine boy. The children grew and became lovely youth and were loved by their stepfather as his own. I was shocked to hear several years ago that the older girl, a beautiful cheerleader, also became pregnant while in high school. Like mother, like daughter. "The fathers have eaten sour grapes, and the children's teeth are set on edge" (Ezek. 18:2).

Poverty Cycle

Many times youth become pregnant simply to get out of the home. They feel if they can marry and have a baby, they can leave their parents. The hope is nourished that the husband will take care of the girl and give her nice things. The tragedy of this is that very few teenage marriages work. The guilt, the financial difficulties, the lack of education, the shortage of emotional maturity, and the inevitable storms are characteristics which cause six out of ten teenage marriages to end in divorce within five years. Seven out of ten will go on welfare.

Breakdown of Values and Standards

One of the sad happenings in our country is the lack of standards. Divorce used to be a stigma; teenage pregnancy used to be a scourge. Not anymore. We don't cry over sin like we used to. We're not burdened over sin like we used to be. People don't know how to blush and be ashamed anymore. That's why we see 94 percent of the sexual situations on television being between unmarried people. There is a tremendous erosion of the home and the church. We have reached the place where bad is good, and good is bad. Movie stars and entertainers tell us this. Sin is not considered wrong anymore. The home and the body are not sacred to the society in which we live.

Unsupervised Time

Experts from several organizations have echoed this reason. Our teenagers today are having more unsupervised time than they have ever had. There is the situation of the working mother. Many of these mothers are single-handedly rearing the family and cannot be present at critical times. Do you know where most pregnancies are being conceived? Perhaps at home in the beds of the parents! Do you know when most of the pregnancies are being conceived? Not in the late hours of the night but maybe between 3:00 and 5:00 in the afternoon! I have known good parents who have gone away from home for a week and left a seventeen-year-old boy there. The house is available with no supervision. Teenagers are having it all laid out there for them, and it is too much temptation.

Eroticized Society

Teenagers are being bombarded today by sexual suggestions and allurements throughout society. Everything the teenager reads, buys, sees, and hears is punctuated by eroticism. Their minds and passions are constantly inflamed by a society totally out of control.

The Cure for Teen Pregnancy

I want to approach the cure for teenage pregnancy in two ways. First, I want to deal with it as if the girl is pregnant; what should we do now? But also I want to deal with the cure from the aspect of prevention. The marriage bed should never be defiled! We should work on keeping our teenagers pure—keep Humpty-Dumpty from falling off the wall!

If the Teenager Is Pregnant

What counsel do we give?

The possibility of marriage.—Very possibly, one of the first and best options is for the couple to be married. Do understand that I suggest this only as a possibility. It would be wonderful if the girl had a mate, and the baby could be born with an acknowledged father. There are so many qualifications here, however, and I honestly have not seen many teen pregnancies end up in good marriages. Most of the time the baby was not conceived in love, and two wrongs do not make a right. A baby is one of the acid tests of any marriage, especially where the partners are children themselves. The Lord would have to be in both of their lives, and they would have to understand the purpose and potential of the marriage relationship.

The marriage of a teen couple will be hard, especially with a baby. I heard a mother tell her daughter: "Your Saturday morning sleep-ins are over. As a matter of fact, your whole nights of sleep are finished. If you won't feed the dog now, what makes you think you'll feed a baby all the times a little one requires?" Strong but straight advice.

The relationship of the couple changes with the addition of a baby. I mean, she used to sit on his lap, but now there's a baby between them. The girl used to be able to go places in a jiffy, but when pregnant or with a small baby, she is immobile and vulnerable. There are strains on the teenage relationship which forces them to grow up—fast! All too often, since the young father has trouble coping, he may resort to flight, leaving his wife and baby to fend for himself as he is "out with the boys" or dodging his responsibility at home. Of course, there are cases where the young husband and wife assume equal responsibility, but those cases seem to be in the minority.

I do not say that marriage is a possibility in many cases, but in some instances it works. Age, maturity, Christian stature, finances, and parental support are some of the factors which should be considered.

Have the baby and not marry.—Ninety percent of the teenagers end up keeping the baby. Much of the success of a girl being able to keep and rear the baby depends on the girl's mother. The teen's mother is crucial. If you have a mother who can and will help, much of the pressure is taken from the teen mother. She may then be able to continue her education and/or land a job. If the mother cannot or is not willing to help, then the teen mother has potential problems. The job, living expenses, housing, child care, and medical bills are almost insurmountable to a teen mother without the support of her family. We must keep in mind that, if the girl does not marry the father, the chances of his providing support is almost nil.

Put the baby up for adoption.—Many cases are seeing this as the most viable possibility. However, the mother's instinct emerges, even from a teenager, and sometimes blocks this possibility. Many times this is overwhelmingly the best solution because the baby is assured of a good home and upbringing. We have many folks in our church who have adopted babies and are outstanding families. Read your Bible and see how many outstanding people were from adopted families, and God blessed and used them.

There are many excellent organizations who will work with you in arranging for the adoption of the baby. Many church agencies are available to help in this matter—also state and private organizations. Look carefully into the reputation of such an agency before you make a final decision. One of the positive points about this position is that the baby is will probably be assured of a good home.

Abortion.—The last suggestion is *no suggestion!* I realize abortion will go through a teen's mind: *My parents will never know. This will just be between me and my doctor.* No, an abortion goes deeper than that. Abortion is murder—"Thou shalt not kill." That baby is alive in the mother, and we should never advocate abortion except in the rarest cases where the life of the living mother is threatened. You ask, "What about rape or incest?" The baby is still alive! What if people like the late, great singer Ethel Waters had been aborted? How tragic the loss to the world would have been if Miss Waters's mother had aborted her little baby. Psalm 139:13-16 shows that God knows us while we are in our mother's womb. The prophet, Jeremiah, was known by God while he was yet unborn (Jer. 1:5). Do not even think about abortion!

Prevention

If a youth is pregnant, there are only three alternatives: Have the baby and get married; have and rear the baby without marriage; have the baby and put the baby up for adoption

The greatest cure which we should concentrate is that of prevention. If a pregnancy occurs, the family and church must move in redemptive efforts to salvage the lives of the mother and baby. However, what can we do to prevent teenage pregnancy from ever happening?

Distinguish differences.—We need to educate our teens about the differences between them. There are crucial physical, emotional, and sexual differences between boys and girls which should be explained carefully and prayerfully to the teens several times at key occasions. Some boys are dominated by pleasure, curiosity, and by peer pressure in their sexual desires. A girl is dominated by the need for security and acceptance. Many boys are "hit and run," while some girls are looking for a meaningful relationship. However, we cannot stereotype boys and girls in these matters.

Teenagers do not understand the dangers of petting. Petting leads to more petting which leads to frustration and, sometimes, to an explosion of uncontrollable passion. The time to say "no" is before passion runs out of control: Make your commitment to Christ and stand by it.

Wisdom of waiting.—Youth normally think in the present tense—"now." A cure for teenage pregnancy is for youth to learn about the wisdom of waiting. They must be taught to wait on God to send them the right person. They must wait for those desires to be channeled in God's way. As parents, we must teach them, encourage them, and pray for them to wait for God's best.

I heard Miss America of 1984, Charlene Wells, interviewed. I was so impressed by her convictions concerning love, dating, sexuality, and marriage. She testified that she had kept herself all those years for the right fellow so that they might be one in marriage. Miss Wells remarked that she had never been ashamed to meet old boy friends, because she knew she has been pure all those years. Her advice to teens was for them to look down the road and consider the consequences. Make up your mind before you go out on a date. Above all, wait until marriage to be intimate with someone.

Parent's pattern.—Our youth often are not receiving good signals from their parents. When they don't see Daddy around and when they see Mother not satisfied, their own convictions are weakened. When the parents are not close to the Lord, the children have no protection or security. A vicious cycle begins to take shape: broken homes produce broken children who produce broken marriages who produce broken homes with broken children, and the like. Our fathers and mothers must return to the examples set forth in the Scriptures (Eph. 5:22-33).

Peace of purity.—Somewhere in life a person must accept God's Word as his standard for conduct. We remember the Seventh Commandment is: "Thou shalt not commit adultery" (Ex. 20:14). Hebrews 13:4 says the marriage bed is not to be defiled. The Bible says God will judge someone who is a whoremonger and an adulterer. Do we believe that?

First Thessalonians 4:3 says: "For this is the will of God, even your sanctification, that ye should abstain from fornication." Do we want to do God's will? Then, we should abstain from sexual sins. Our bodies belong to God and our future mate. Paul asked Timothy to be an example of the believer in word, conversation, charity, spirit, faith, and purity (1 Tim. 4:12). We are not to be conformed to this world (Rom. 12:2). The Christian is to dress modestly (1 Tim. 2:19). Live for God! Be pure.

Do you remember at the first of this chapter I talked about a major television program dealing with teenage pregnancy? At the close of that program, they interviewed a strikingly beautiful young girl. The first scene showed only her, but then the camera panned away to reveal a little child in her arms. The one conducting the interview asked her, "If you could redesign your life, what would you have done differently?" And, there on nationwide television, this lovely girl replied: "I'd stay a virgin. If I could do it over, I'd stay a virgin."

And if she had stayed a virgin and had waited for God to bring His best to her:

- She would be married to a man that God led to her.
- They would have had the precious experience together of bringing a life into the world.
- There would be no affliction of deep scars and regrets from her youth.
- She would look forward to meeting her husband each day as he came home.
- Her heart would trust in him knowing that he would not be flirting or being immoral while away from her.
- She would thrill seeing her husband play with their daughter each night.

All of this would have been hers if she had remained a virgin and obediently waited for God to direct her life. The list of thrills for the Christian is endless. May God bless our young people!

5

What Should I Do When . . . I Am Sick?

One of the most godly women I have ever known or pastored contracted cancer. This dear woman had never smoked, drunk any alcoholic beverages, or used drugs. Her life centered around her family and church. She and her husband reared four spiritual children, one of whom entered the ministry. Every revival found us at her house for the final Sunday meal, and the speciality was always sweet and sour pork! When this woman became terminally ill, my faith was shaken. As a family and as a church, all of us went through proper spiritual channels (as we then understood prayer and faith), but our friend died. I remember so vividly arriving at the hospital and seeing the effects of cancer upon her lifeless body. I remember thinking: *Lord, could we have prevented this? Is there something we are missing in faith or prayer that could have saved this dear saint's life?*

This experience and others prompted me to pray, study, and preach about physical healing. Another outstanding woman in our church also was stricken with cancer. Over the years, she has suffered in her fight for life. One of our young men spoke to her husband and earnestly urged him to call for the elders of the church that they might pray for his wife. The husband replied to the sincere young deacon: "Naw, I don't believe in all that hocus-pocus."

I can still see the young deacon's face and hear the disbelief in his voice: "Pastor, he called prayer for the sick a bunch of hocus-pocus! He's going to sit there and let his wife die!"

It is an indictment upon my denomination, I feel. In my continued search for answers concerning physical illness and faith, I contacted my brethren around Middle Tennessee. I asked various denominational leaders if any churches were known to have special prayer for the sick. Did any churches lay hands on the sick and anoint them with oil? The answer was "no."

I had to call non-Baptists to see who had the faith to obey the Scriptures concerning a genuine ministry to the sick. There were two well-known non-Baptist churches in the Nashville area, renowned for their faith in prayer and exercise of spiritual gifts. I called the first church and asked to talk to the pastor about their ministry to the sick. What a coincidence! The pastor was home—sick!

I then called the second church and asked to talk to the pastor. This pastor was most gracious and shared with me willingly for the next hour. How refreshing to hear his faith and child-like obedience to the Word of God. He related how his church regularly practiced specific prayer, laying on of hands, and the anointing of the sick. This church's ministry did not "smack of hocus-pocus," and I rejoiced in hearing many answers to prayer. My pastor friend on the telephone left me with this thought: "The point is, Billie, we have done what we believe to be the will of God according to the Scriptures. The healing is in God's hands and left to Him. We have been obedient."

The subject of divine healing has been a mystery to most Christians in general and to my people particular. Television ministries have made it controversial and comical. The potential of a specific ministry to the sick has been abused as Satan has covered it with mistaken ideas. I went to my Bible and found that Jesus had a threefold ministry: teaching, preaching, and healing (Matt. 4:23-25). When our Lord called His twelve disciples, He "gave them power against unclean spirits, to cast them out, and to *heal all manner of sickness* and *all manner of disease*" (Matt. 10:1, author's italics). The disciples became supernatural extensions of Christ and continued teaching, preaching, and healing in His name. Should healing be a part of our ministry today?

Are miracles of healing for today? Looking back over the history of church, miracles continued to about A.D. 300, and then mysteriously began to disappear. Why? We hear more of supernatural visitations from our mission fields than we do from our

American churches. Why? I realize the gospel in foreign lands clashes with natural and animalistic religions which almost force contests similar to the Mount Carmel incident (1 Kings 18). But, do our missionaries believe and apply the Word more literally than we do in America?

I meditated much on James 5:13-16 and was haunted by the question: "Is any sick among you?" (v. 14). Of course, I had sickness among my membership! Regularly! Weekly! Devastatingly! It seems as though our sick list each week outnumbers our answers to prayer. My children avoid the news each night because it is always "bad news." Our prayer meetings begin to sound the same way: diseases, illnesses, and sicknesses. Every Wednesday we hear pathology reports about the latest person struck by illness. "Is any sick among you?" Yes! We must do something!

Hopefully you share my concern about wanting to be used of God more adequately in facing the continued crisis of sickness. Every pastor should want to develop some specific spiritual strategies in combating sickness. I have felt like Satan was having a heyday coming into my house (the church), spoiling my goods (the members), and laughing at my impotent defense (the strong man)—Matthew 12:29. Let us consider the characteristics of sickness and treatment, causes of sickness, and cure for sickness.

Characteristics of Sickness

"Is any sick among you?" I researched the words *sick* and *sickness* and found these mentioned fifty-six times in the New Testament. Two main words are used: *astheneo* and *paralutikos*. *Astheneo* is the word used in James 5:14 and is the main word used refering to *sick* in the New Testament. It means without strength, diseased, and impotent.

Let us note three beginning principles.

The Sentence of Death Is in Our Bodies

Sickness is a natural result of human sin. Sorrow, pain, and death were inherited by humans because Adam sinned (Gen. 3:16-19). Now, each person bears in his or her body the inevitability of death. "Wherefore, as by one man sin entered into the world, and death by sin; and so *death passed upon all men,* for that all have sinned" (Rom. 5:12, author's italics). If you live long enough, you will die. The sentence of death is in our bodies.

God prepares us for the execution of that sentence. Paul wrote that the outward body perishes (2 Cor. 4:16). This word *perish* means to come to ruin, decay, or rot thoroughly. Is that not what is happening to our bodies as we age? In 1 Corinthians 15:53, Paul describes our bodies as "corruptible." This word is related to the word *perish* (*diaphtheiro*). The definition of *corruptible (phtheiro)* so suits one's preparation for death—to wither, shrivel, or spoil. A picture provided for us in the Bible of the withering, shriveling process happening in our bodies can be found in Ecclesiastes 12:3-7.

The presence of sickness accompanies the result of sin's curse. "Is any sick among you?" The writer knew there would be because of the nature of humans. I shall never forget a conversation I had with a doctor, during the illness of our first child. Although Christa only had the croup, as new parents we imagined it much worse. I watched this little child cough, shiver, and toss in her sleep. Righteous indignation built up in me, and I lashed out at the doctor: "Why does this little baby have to get sick? I wish I could fight sickness out on the parking lot, and it would never show its face around her again! I don't understand why this little girl has to be sick!"

The doctor, a Christian and a wise man, calmly counseled, "Brother Billie, if Christa doesn't get sick, she will never develop any immunities." That was not the answer I wanted to hear, but it surely stopped my righteous tirade! We will get sick because the sentence of death is in our bodies.

God Has Prescribed the Limits of a Normal Life Span

The earlier point probably came across as bad news to you. But, cheer up! God will give each of us enough time to fulfill our mission on earth. Usually that can be done within the time span of seventy years: "The days of our years are threescore years and ten" (Ps. 90:10). Our bodies seem to be designed like an alarm clock: We begin to wind down and head home at around seventy. We should accept aging and death as inevitable. I believe the best is always yet to be.

God is in charge of our lives. He has "determined the times before appointed, and the bounds of their habitation" (Acts 17:26). Rather than be pessimistic and negative about the presence of illness, let us put our lives in the hands of a loving and almighty God. Your life, with its purpose and timing, was set by an all-knowing Father in heaven. Esther doubted her purpose in life, but Mordecai encouraged her: "Who knoweth whether thou art come to the kingdom for such a time as this?" (Esth. 4:14). God does have a plan and purpose for our lives, and He will give us the time on earth to fulfill that plan. "So teach us to number our days, that we may apply our hearts unto wisdom" (Ps. 90:12).

We Should Live a Healthy Life-style

Knowing that we are born with a purpose to fulfill, we should aspire to care for our bodies. We are always thrilled beyond words when a senior adult is saved. However, I am saddened that he can only present to Christ a broken-down body for service. This is why we urge people to be saved as children and youth: "while the evil days come not" (Eccl. 12:1). How we should want our bodies to be vessels unto "honor, sanctified, and meet for the master's use, and prepared unto every good work"! (2 Tim. 2:21).

Did you know most of the major destructive diseases are preventable? Many of the heart diseases, cancer, and other sicknesses relate to our style of living—and they are based on our choices! We choose to overeat, smoke cigarettes, drink alcohol, avoid exercise, and keep long hours. Knowing we are created in the image of God (Gen. 1:27) with the Holy Spirit indwelling us (1 Cor. 6:19), each of us should "know how to possess his vessel in sanctification and honor" (1 Thess. 4:4).

Causes of Sickness

"Is any sick among you?" Because the fall brought the possibilities of sickness and death to every person, a healthy person is probably an accident waiting to happen! One might say a healthy person is simply one whose opportunistic germs have not yet been activated or whose diseases are in remission. A man went to his doctor for a complete physical. After the tests were completed, the doctor told his patient; "You are as sound as a dollar." The man fainted! (The dollar, of course, is not that sound these days). Most of us are more sound than the dollar most of the time. But, occasionally, our bodies break down, and we "catch something." Germs seem to be in the air.

My wife's doctor had several patients with miscarriages in one week a few years ago. When questioned about it, he replied, "Something was just going through Nashville."

We do not want to be overly simplistic, but this section will deal with the causes of sickness based on the Bible. We do not have enough time or space to deal with all the physical causes of sickness treated by more than 7,000 American hospitals. Each of the 1.6 million hospital beds was filled practically every day, since more than 20 percent of all Americans spent time in the hospital. We also know that millions were treated on an out-patient basis. The phrase, "Is any sick among you?"becomes more profound and provocative in its implications the more we think about it!

For all the many diagnosed sicknesses, we believe there to be only three causes as announced from the Bible:

Sickness for the Glory of God

The first classification of sicknesses deals with those illnesses that we contract, pray about, receive treatment for, are made well of, and give glory to God. Jesus, when asked about Lazarus, said, "This sickness is not unto death, but for the *glory of God,* that the Son of God might be *glorified* thereby" (John 11:4, author's italics). The final result of Lazarus's sickness was not death, but the glory of God. Sometimes God permits sickness in order to reveal His glory.

The man born blind in John 9 is another example. The disciples asked if his blindness was a result of his sin or the sin of his parents. Jesus answered, "Neither hath this man sinned, nor his parents: but that the works of God should be made manifest in him" (v. 3). Christ looks to the future not to the past. The blindness gave opportunity for God's power to be shown.

Some sickness comes upon us and God can use it for His glory. Paul, who had his share of affliction, testified: "Therefore will I rather glory in my infirmities, that the power of Christ may rest upon me" (2 Cor. 12:9). While we know God's perfect will would be that no one ever suffer, infirmities do come to the children of God because of sin's effects. These times can lead us to pray, come closer to God, and humble ourselves. As we overcome these trials, God receives glory. Have we learned our lessons in suffering?

Sickness Because of Sin

Some sickness may come as a judgment upon sin, a form of chastisement. Paul, addressing a problem about the Lord's Supper at Corinth, stated that sin had caused many to be "weak" and "sickly among you" (1 Cor. 11:30). These terms refer to sickness and illness. We know that, if a person sows to the flesh, he or she will reap "corruption" (Gal. 6:8). This is the same word we mentioned earlier showing how the body deteriorates with age (*phtheiro*—as found in 1 Cor. 15:54). When we sow to the flesh and not to the Spirit, our bodies are affected. Chastisement can take the form of illness or a ruinous effect upon the body.

The Bible contains many vivid examples of sickness coming because of sin. Miriam, Moses' sister, was struck with leprosy because of rebellion toward God's leadership (Num. 12:9-10). Uzziah was a great king until pride produced sinful presumption on his part to burn incense on the Lord's altar. He was struck by the Lord with leprosy and was cut off from the Lord's house until the day of his death (2 Chron. 26:16-21).

I believe that many of our devastating diseases today are results of breaking God's laws. Romans 1 talks about the sin of homosexuality. God hates the homosexuality but loves the homosexual person. However, there is a built-in chastisement to this sin: "men with men working that which is unseemly, and *receiving in themselves* that recompense of *their error* which was meet" (v. 27, author's italics). Sexual sins bring chastisement upon the body.

Sickness unto Death

Eventually, all will die or be translated at the Lord's return. Hebrews 9:27 says, "And as it is appointed unto men once to die, but after this the judgment." There may come that sickness unto death that carries a person into eternity. When that sickness comes, no doctor, hospital, or medicine can stop God's action—one goes home!

The life of Elisha illustrates the sickness unto death. We remember how wonderful the life and ministry of Elisha was: Miracles and mighty works attended his time on earth. Elisha was used by God to bring back to life the son of the Shunammite woman (2 Kings 4:32-37). This mighty prophet was the one instrumental in the marvelous healing of Naaman (2 Kings 5). However, with mixed emotions we read 2 Kings 13:14, "Now Elisha was fallen sick of his sickness whereof he died." Although Elisha had prayer power and walked with God, there came a time when sickness came which could not be healed. It was that sickness unto death.

I watched an interesting Christian program on television one night. A panel of outstanding faith healers was being interviewed. Soon, the moderator commented, "Now, guys, we know that all of our prayers have not been answered. We have to admit that we've had close family and friends we prayed for, and yet they died. How do we explain that?" The consensus answer was that perfect healing may take place for some only in heaven. We pray for everyone, but the ultimate answer is in the hands of God. We never know when a sickness may be the one unto death that brings us home to God.

The Cure for Sickness

"Is any among you sick?" What a question! We know there are those among us who are sick. The question is not if we will be sick, but "What should I do when I am sick?"

Over the years, there have been three main routes humans have taken when sickness came to their lives:

No Prayer—No Faith

This is when the person and his or her family would rely totally on the medical doctor and the treatment. Probably, this idea prevails more in Christendom than we realize. I doubt seriously whether many Christians instinctively look to God when illness comes. We automatically think of the doctor and begin to pull out our checkbook. You will remember the time a sick woman came to Jesus who had endured an issue of blood for twelve years. The Bible says she "had spent all her living upon physicians, neither could be healed of any" (Luke 8:43). She had concentrated only on earthly doctors and had never made a spiritual advance toward the Great Physician.

All Prayer—All Faith

This position is held by a few people who go to the other extreme. These folks sincerely place all their faith in God to the exclusion of any man-made methods. In Tennessee, there was a case several years ago where a girl had cancer in her leg. Her parents devoutly believed in spiritual healing and abhorred man-made methods. This particular case achieved such notoriety that the lawyers and doctors forced the hospitalization of the girl for treatment. While we admire the sincere faith of people taking this position, we do not believe the correct conduct should be "either-or" but "both-and."

Blending of the Two

I propose a blending of these two positions. Let us, first of all, admit and believe that all healing is of God. Let us pray with all of our hearts for God's miraculous healing power to be applied to the situation. But, also, let us use all of the God-given means for treatment.

There is no question that God is treating the sick today through hospitals, doctors, and nurses. Many of these people may not be Christians, but they are God's instruments. We contend that the research, the knowledge, and the techniques are gifts from God to the medical profession. The surgery may cut out a piece of tissue, but if the condition were to be left as the surgeons finished the operation, the wound would never heal. Even an unsaved surgeon lives by faith that healing will take place. Life does the healing, and God sends life. A person may tend broken, sick bodies, but only God can mend them. The good Samaritan bound up the wounds of the injured man, but only God could heal them (Luke 10:34).

Practical Suggestions

Some things I suggest to do when you are sick are as follows:

Determine the Type of Sickness

Your sickness could be one of three types: sickness for God's glory, sickness because of sin, or a sickness unto death. Through prayer and abiding in the Word of God, you can determine which type you have. If you have a sickness because of sin—ask God to forgive you and seek to make reconciliation with the involved people, if possible. Forgiveness and cleansing should bring restoration and healing. If the sickness is for God's glory, commit your condition to God and know He will not put more on you than you can bear (1 Cor. 10:13). God's grace will be sufficient (2 Cor. 12:9). If this is a sickness unto death, God's dying grace will not come until you need it. He will be with you. We have shown our children how to live—now, let us show them how to die. A man in my church remarked how we don't see death-bed experiences any more. In former days, children saw their parents leave this world and received encouragement as God provided dying grace. Today, we have our people so taped up, tubed up, and tanked up on medication that death-bed experiences are about extinct.

Follow the Instructions in James 5:13-16

Pray (v. 13).—Really pray. Determine the type of sickness you have and act accordingly. Until you know differently, ask God to remove this affliction. Until He does, learn from it. Be sensitive to His leadership from His Word. (John 15:7).

Call for the elders of the church (v. 14).—*Elders* are *presbuteros* and refer in James's day to the bearded ones, wise, and experienced ones in the faith. These should have the Christian characteristics of maturity, faith, and fullness in Christ. Today, the elders would refer to the church staff, deacons, and/or spiritual church leaders—people whom we trust to pray over us.

Notice that the involvement of the church leaders is totally at the initiative of the sick person. The church leaders do not volunteer their participation—the burden must originate within the soul and faith of the one in need. The sick person has recognized one's need and has faith beginning to operate in one's heart to the extent that he or she obeys the Word. The sick person is ready to submit to God through the church leaders. I really believe this must be taught in our churches so that people know what the Bible says and think spiritually when such an occasion arises.

Submit to the elders (v. 14).—Faith is operating in the heart of the sick person. The Scripture is obeyed as the church leaders are called. These leaders represent God. The sick person should submit to them as they do the following:

Pray over the sick person (v. 14).—The term, "pray over him," can refer to several things: (1) Stretch hands toward the person in prayer; (2) Stretch hands over the person in prayer; (3) Place hands on the person during the prayer; (4) Stand over the person when praying; or, (5) It could refer to a prayer of authority as the sick person submits to God through the elders.

Anoint with oil (v. 14).—This point has been a source of controversy over the years as to the exact purpose of the oil. There are two main words for *anoint*. One word is a*leiphoo*—translated to rub, massage, or to oil. This word is found in Luke 7:38 as Jesus' feet were washed with the woman's tears and anointed with fragrant oil. The word is also found in Mark 16:1 where the women came to the tomb to anoint Jesus' body. This word is never used in sacred or religious usage—it is not the word in James 5:14! The other word is *chrioo* and is used in Luke 4:18 where Jesus says: "The Spirit of the Lord is upon me, because he hath anointed me to preach the gospel." In Acts 4:27, Jesus is called the "holy, anointed servant." This word is the one used by the passage in James 5:14. It appears to be a spiritual, not practical word for "anoint."

The oil could be used as *medicine.* The good Samaritan used oil as a healing element on the injured man's wounds. Mark 6:13 says the disciples "anointed with oil many that were sick": This word is *aleiphoo* and implies a medicinal usage. The oil could also be seen as *symbolic* of God's presence and power. We know oil in the Scriptures symbolizes the Holy Spirit and was used to anoint kings. Or, the oil could be an actual *vehicle for God's Word.* As one anoints, one is being obedient to the Word of God. We are a "doer of the Word" (Jas. 1:22).

Says prayer for faith (v. 15).—Notice that the oil does not heal, but

God answers the prayer of faith. The prayer of faith comes from an uncondemning heart (1 John 3:21-22; Ps. 66:18), recognizes the will of God (1 John 5:14), rests on the promise of Christ (Mark 11:24), and invokes the name of Jesus (Jas. 5:14; John 14:13-14; Luke 10:17; Acts 3:6). The name of Jesus embraces our Lord's character, authority, and power.

Walk by faith.—Claim the Word. "As ye have therefore received Christ Jesus the Lord, so walk ye in him" (Col. 2:6). God will reveal His will to you and then give you the ability to do His will (Phil. 2:13).

Let God lead you to a Christian doctor.—Take your medicine with prayer. There are doctors who believe in prayer and miracles and who walk in God's will. Ask your pastor or a godly friend about Christian doctors in the area. One of America's most famous evangelists canceled a revival with us to care for his wife. He had prayed fervently, but he reached a point where he entrusted her to the care of wise physicians.

Believe God!—Feed your faith on God's Word! Meditate on great verses of Scripture and visualize God working in your body. "With men this is impossible; but with God all things are possible" (Matt. 19:26). I repeat: Feed your faith! (Heb. 11:6; Rom. 10:17).

Glorify God with your life.—Carry out any vows you make. God lengthened Hezekiah's life, but it would have been better if Hezekiah had died at God's first notice. He did not glorify God with his lengthened life (2 Kings 20). Be faithful to God with your life. Perform your vows (Eccl. 5:2-6).

Do you remember Asa in the Bible? God used him in many wonderful works, but the end of his life is sad. "And Asa in the thirty and ninth year of his reign was diseased in his feet, until his disease was exceeding great." How do you think Asa responded to this crisis? "Yet in his disease he sought not to the Lord, but to the physicians" (2 Chron. 16:12). If there is a thesis to this chapter, it is let us seek God *first* when we are sick! Let us pray specifically. Let us learn to use our faith. Let us obey the Scriptures as God reveals them to us.

6

What Should I Do When . . . I Lose My Job?

I felt so sorry for the man who sat in front of me. "I just don't know what I'm going to do, Preacher," he groaned. His nervous hands never stopped moving as he explained his situation. "I've felt it coming for a while now with computers and machines being brought in and guys being laid off. I thought that, with twelve years of service, I would miss the layoffs. But, last week they gave me my walking papers." The distraught husband and father proceeded to give me his financial picture and hopes for the future. The company offered him another job, he mentioned, but it would mean relocating in another state. What should he do? He had a family depending on him.

Every pastor has had the question posed to him: "What should I do when I lose my job?" Personally, there are few crises affecting a family which disturb me more than when the husband (or wife) loses his job. Work is the central activity in the lives of most people. Work provides an income, an identity, and a structure around which other activities revolve. Almost 40 percent of a person's time on Monday through Friday is concerned with the job. Almost 25 percent of the entire week focuses around one's career. The job is important to the person and the family!

There are more than 100 million people in America who work for a living. All have one thing in common: They could lose their jobs. This traumatic experience could happen to any of us—no one is exempt! Each of us should begin making plans right now on how to cope with this devastating emergency. This year one in every four workers will experience some type of season of unemployment—that is 25 percent of America. Millions of Americans now holding jobs cannot have any confidence that the skills they possess will assure them continued employment.

It was Jacob who originally said, "And now when shall I provide for mine own house also?" (Gen. 30:30). One of the famous patriarchs expressed concern as to how he would provide for his family. We, too, are concerned for our friends and Christian family who lose their source of income and provision. We sincerely hope this chapter will help one find God's direction in facing the crisis of being out of work.

We will divide the study into these parts: the consideration of work, causes of job loss, consequences of job loss, and the cure for job loss.

Consideration of Work

In Ephesians 4:28, we find the "Three Stages of Civilization": "Let him that stole steal no more: but rather let him labor, working with his hands the thing which is good, that he may have to give to him that needeth." Do you see the stages of civilization? One may *steal* to get what one needs—this is dishonorable, of course, and not God's will. How honorable it is to *labor* to attain one's needs. Notice that the labor should be "good." One of the blessings of labor is that one is able to *give* (the highest stage of civilization) from what one earns to help others in need. One of our goals in life should be to reach the point where our needs are met, and we are able to help others. From Ephesians 4:28, note these characteristics of our work:

- Our job should *bring income* to our family.
- Our job should *provide security* for our family.
- Our job should be a *ministry* in our lives.
- Our job should *bring satisfaction* to our lives.

In our consideration of work, let us see what the Scriptures say about the Christian and his vocation:

Work Is Expected

Work should be done by everyone. In the garden of Eden, Adam was given a job (Gen. 2:15). He was told after the fall that he would earn his bread by the sweat of his face (3:19). Thomas Edison, who said "Genius is 1 percent inspiration and 99 percent perspiration," loved to work. His wife tried to get him to take a vacation, to no avail. One day she told him to think about the place where he'd like to be more than any other place in the world. She told him to go there the next morning. Sure enough, the next morning she found him at work in his beloved laboratory! Work is to be expected of persons by God.

God Is Interested in Our Work and Worship

The same Commandment telling us to worship also tells us to work (Ex. 20:8-11). We know God is interested in what we put in the collection plate—He is also interested in how the money comes into our hands. To that end, God says: "Six days shalt thou labor, and do all thy work" (Ex. 20:9). Worship is more meaningful when we have obeyed in working during the week.

We Should Give Our Best When Working

The ant is used as an example to us in Proverbs 6:6-11. The ant has no laziness but conducts its business with wisdom, efficiency, and industriousness. People are told that poverty will come to them unless they emulate the example of the ant (vv. 9-11). "Slothfulness casteth into a deep sleep; and an idle soul shall suffer hunger" (19:15). Every Christian should do one's best at his or her job: "Whatsoever thy hand findeth to do, do it with thy might" (Eccl. 9:10).

Work Is Therapeutic

Work is never harmful! Only worry and tension will wear one down. I heard about a man who loved to work so much that his wife took him to the psychiatrist. He was diagnosed as a workaholic and now must take a second job to pay for the treatments! Work purifies a person and makes one happy: The unhappy people are those who consume much and contribute little. "The sleep of a laboring man is sweet, whether he eat little or much" (Eccl. 5:12). The wise man also said, "Every man should eat and drink, and enjoy the good of all his labor, it is the gift of God" (Eccl. 3:13). Yes, work enables a person to sleep soundly at night and enjoy one's food. A secret of those who live long is they had good work habits. Wouldn't you rather wear out than rust out?

Our Work Should Be Honest

Surely it goes without saying that our work should be honest and in keeping with God's law. A servant is urged by Paul to "obey in all things your masters" (Col. 3:22). We are to earn our money honestly. God's leaders are not to be "greedy of filthy lucre" (1 Tim. 3:3,8). We will reap what we sow and in proportion to what we sow (Gal. 6:7-8). Jeremiah has a word for our day: "Woe unto him that buildeth his house by unrighteousness, and his chambers by wrong; that useth his neighbour's service without wages, and giveth him not for his work" (Jer. 22:13). I have known men who had greedy hearts. Honest work was not enough for them. They suffered disgrace and even imprisonment.

Our Work Should Be Holy

Does your work satisfy you? Do you feel a dignity, a value, and a holy compensation as your work is done well? A man applied for a job as a prison guard. "Any experience?" asked the personnel director.

"Well," the man answered, "I did drive a school bus for nine years!" His job had no dignity: He saw it as a prison!

Our labor in this life is not just to live better here. Our labor is not just to save for rainy day. Our labor in this life is not just to leave behind things for our relatives to fight over! Do you remember the rich fool in Luke 12:16-21? He forgot others, he forgot God, he forgot his own soul, and he forgot about eternity. What do you want your work to do for you? Go back to Ephesians 4:28. We work in order to have so that we are able to give. Life is too short, and eternity will be too long if we see our work only as "9 to 5." We should worship as we work! (1 Cor. 10:31).

I love my work! I have always enjoyed working. As a boy in Florida, I worked in the fruit and melon industries. I had an uncle who was tough to work for, but I learned from him. Upon going to college, I worked part-time as a meat cutter in the A & P store and enjoyed the variety of that job immensely. Then, God called me to preach. Oh, it is almost a "sin" to be as happy as I am as a pastor: I get to study, preach, teach, counsel, witness, administer, disciple, bury, and marry. I have been where I am since December

1972, and I am just as excited now each morning coming to work as I was the very first day! I have never discussed money because my service is unto the Lord, not to men (Eph. 6:7). Like Snow White's seven dwarfs, I worship and whistle while I work!

Causes of Job Loss

Not all Americans are happily fulfilling their mission in life through their work. Many are out of jobs. As a matter of fact, I heard a leader on television say our country has over ten million people now looking for work. He said about 60 percent of that figure represented men out of work.

Why would people lose their jobs?

Poor Performance

There are some people out of work because they could not meet the company's standards. The usual reason is not that they couldn't do the work, but wouldn't do the work! Inefficient work habits, laziness, inability to follow directions, and dishonesty may be grounds for which a person is terminated from one's employment. We are not to give our service with "eye-service, as men-pleasers; but as the servants of Christ, doing the will of God from the heart" (Eph. 6:6).

Prejudice of Employers

Occasionally, our Christian convictions will meet with animosity from a non-Christian employer. Joseph made his employer a rich man but lost his job through a situation where he stood on his godly convictions (Gen. 39:1-20). We remember that Daniel was a wonderful employee and was honored for his work. However, envy from his colleagues (Dan. 6:4-5) caused him to be thrown into the lions' den. As a pastor, I have had godly men whose jobs were threatened by non-Christian employers. Their job performances were not in question, but their social customs and morality were seen as threats by ungodly employers.

Company Shutdowns

In the past ten years, our country has seen some gigantic company shut-downs. When I was in Louisiana, one of the world's largest, sulphur mines business dropped drastically because of foreign competition. While in Nashville, many of my members have been laid off from renowned companies. Sometimes shrinking output caused the collapse. Other times, the company saw relocation to another state as in its best interest. People's lives are tremendously affected by changes in large companies. In some places, the city becomes a ghost town after the main business collapses.

Skill Deficiency

What advances we have seen in the technology of America's businesses! This truly has become the computer-laser-nuclear age. Many people find their skills are not proficient enough for the way the company is progressing. Low-skill positions are being replaced by jobs requiring more extensive education and training. Economists predict three out of four jobs in the future will require education and training beyond the high school level. And, how does this compare with the functional illiteracy of more than 23 million adults in America? Also, what will happen to the more than one million high school students who drop out each year? And, to compound this point even more, more than one million teenagers become pregnant each year. Half of these are rearing their children as single parents. Half of these mothers will not graduate from high school. As a result, three-fourths of all single mothers under twenty-five are living in poverty.

Let me pursue the implications of this point for a moment. As our economy grows, jobs will be created. However, the high-paying jobs will require specialized skills and extensive education. There always has been (and is presently) an abundance of jobs, but the catch is they are in service industry areas where the pay is near minimum wage with little or no benefits. These are jobs in restaurants, hotels, and retail sales work. Single mothers and family leaders will not be able to survive on minimum wage to meet soaring rent, utility, and food costs.

Consequences of Job Loss

Most people have no idea how to survive the loss of a job. They do not realize the trauma which is about to begin. Losing a job is like losing a loved one in death: First comes grief and then, as the shock wears off, the economic and emotional impact.

Let us name several consequences of the loss of a job.

Financial Consequences

Let's say the family was financially prepared for the job loss (most are not). They may have unemployment insurance and savings, which they live off of for a while. This proves to be a "fantasy" time as they try to maintain their previous life-style. Soon the crunch hits and changes in life-style begin. Old, expensive pleasures are dropped. Medical insurance may be covered only on the children, with dental services being the first to go. If a comparable job does not come, a position paying less than the previous employment is accepted. Dreams are postponed indefinitely. The financial consequences can be devastating and demeaning.

Emotional Consequences

There is a close link between an individual's sense of personal worth and the work one does. There is a great yearning for recognition and meaning in work. Fathers and mothers want to have respect from their children and hope to provide better things for them.

The loss of a job attacks one's self-esteem. A person begins to feel like a failure. Often the person looking for employment will find rejection. If it occurs often enough, the worker ultimately rejects oneself. Depression and discouragement follow. The person may have horrible thoughts and feelings about oneself. Remember Ahithophel, who lost his job as Absalom's counselor. He became depressed, went home, and hanged himself (2 Sam. 17:23). Our churches should pray regularly for those who are out of work.

Physical Consequences

The loss of a job can have severe physical consequences. Again, we repeat, job loss is comparable to the loss of a loved one. Grief and shock lead the way. Then high blood pressure, hypertension, headaches, stomach distress, and sleepless nights can follow. The person may enter a passive, inactive state where social contacts are cut off. The pastor and spouse of the person involved should be especially attentive to the physical consequences.

Marital Consequences

One's marriage can be affected during the trauma of a job loss. Sometimes the person will become a recluse and forsake those whom he or she loves. Other times, guilt and self-blame makes one sensitive. Tempers may flare. Fights occur. The job loss may force the wife to go to work. At first, the husband is grateful for the additional income, but gratitude can turn to hostility over being left at home to care for the children and do housework. The man has not only lost his status as a breadwinner, but has been forced into what he considers a female role. Today, it is not uncommon to find homes with the woman as the main financial support and the man assuming the role of caring for the home.

While these are the primary consequences, there are several more worth mentioning. *Early retirement* can seem more acceptable ego-wise than being unemployed. Also, *temporary jobs* may be taken. Usually these jobs are compensated in cash and do not last very long. They do, however, provide additional needed finances and serve to satisfy one's need for being productive.

The Cure for Job Loss

Practical Suggestions

When a person loses his job, he becomes confused and fearful. A person's life becomes out of focus. How needful for the ministry of the church at a time like this! Let me offer some practical suggestions for your consideration.

Continued money flow.—Financial experts urge us to have at least six months salary in savings for just a time as this. Most are not prepared financially for a job loss. Where would your money come from during the time it takes to find another job? Let me list three sources.

Unemployment insurance.—Most states offer twenty-six weeks of unemployment insurance. This is usually based on the previous earnings and length of employment.

Private benefits.—Your company may have had a pension plan from which you can take your deserved money. There may be a profit-sharing plan from which you receive benefits. Also, you may have severance pay coming to you.

Borrowing.—Resort to this only if the first two do not produce enough. It is important to live within a tight budget during jobless periods. Borrowing means money must be repaid with interest, making the readjustment all the harder. There also may be permanent life insurance policies that can be used.

Stretch reduced income as far as possible.—See your creditors and arrange a payment plan. Don't dodge them! If you are carrying excess baggage in the form of luxuries, be ruthless. Toss them overboard. Have a garage sale. Eat at home.

Call a family council.—Pray about the situation, and then call a serious family council. Try to explain to the family what has happened. Ask for their cooperation. Support one another. Do not cast any blame. Watch out for quarreling and guilt-dumping. This is a great growing time for the family as you pull together for a common need. Expect God to work miracles! Lift up God as your Source during your time of need. Your children will learn through this a great lesson of faith and how God provides for His own.

Your job search.—Don't panic. Keep your resume short and deliver it in person. Check the newspapers and be on the street early. A high percentage of people hired by businesses are recommended by other workers in the organization, so give your name to friends, former coworkers, and colleagues. They will hear of openings sooner than you will.

Spiritual preparation.—These really come before the others. I am listing them at the last to give emphasis to them. I really view these more importantly than the above suggestions:

Acknowledge God's sovereignty.—Have you bowed before God yet? "Promotion cometh neither from the east, nor from the west, nor from the south. But God is the judge: he putteth down one, and setteth up another" (Ps. 75:6-7). I'm telling you, I believe God is in control! He's got the "whole world in His hands." Do you believe this? Your job is waiting for you when you get right with Him. Tell God you are in His hands and want Him to lead.

Pray with an opened Bible.—Seek the Lord. Talk to God as you read your Bible. I believe God will speak to you out of His Word (Ps. 119:105).

Confide in other believers.—Share your burden with the church as you feel led. "In the multitude of counselors, they are established" (Prov. 15:22). I've been in prayer meetings where a person asked God about a job, and a person across the room gave the answer! Don't be bashful or ashamed. Share your burden and concern with your family of faith.

Look for God's lessons.—I really believe God will teach you something through this experience! He will give you comfort and expect you to comfort others by that comfort later (2 Cor. 1:3-4). All things will work together for good (Rom. 8:28). The trying of your faith will produce patience and maturity (Jas. 1:3-4). I expect God to produce patience, perseverance, faithfulness, dependability, and dependence upon Him through this experience. You will probably be closer to Him at this time than any other in life.

Scripture Study

At the close of this chapter, let me share with you a precious word from God given to me at a low time in my life. It is found in Genesis 30—a tremendous study about Jacob. Jacob's life was like a roller coaster—up and down in his devotion with God. He had dreams, visions, and mighty experiences with God. Do you remember his relationship with his father-in-law, Laban? Jacob met his match in Laban! He was tricked into working fourteen years for Leah and Rachel. Laban was blessed by Jacob's employment, too.

Jacob wanted to leave and start living for himself. Every young man is concerned about his family and his fortune. Jacob had done quite well in his family! But, now, he said to his father-in-law: "And now when shall I provide for mine own house also?" (Gen. 30:30). Remember that Jacob and Laban came to one of the most unusual arrangements to be found anywhere in Scripture or literature! Notice the agreements:

- Jacob started with nothing (Gen. 30:31).
- The speckled and spotted sheep were taken out of the herd and moved three days' distance away (vv. 35-36).

• Jacob began only with the solid colors with the agreement being he can claim as his own the speckled and spotted ones in the future (vv. 32-33).

Remember what happened next? Call it prenatal influence or selective breeding, but God begins to bless Jacob. He uses some unorthodox methods (vv. 37-41), but God gives him his required sheep which he continues to selectively breed. The result? "The man increased exceedingly, and had much cattle, and maid-servants, and menservants, and camels, and asses" (v. 43). God blessed Jacob!

Listen! All Jacob wanted was God, plus an opportunity. He did not want anything at the beginning except God (v. 31)! He was willing for his righteousness to answer for him (v. 33). The ingredients for Jacob's success were God's presence, an opportunity, and hard work (31:6). Remember that Jacob started with nothing and still maintained the tithe as he grew (Gen. 28:22).

Have you lost your job? Get ready! You and God are going to have a wonderful adventure and partnership together. All you need is God, an opportunity, and hard work. You can make it! "But seek ye first the kingdom of God, and his righteousness; and all these things shall be added unto you" (Matt. 6:33).

7

What Should I Do When . . . I Am Married to an Unbeliever?

Once there were two sisters who dated two brothers. The girls were Christians and had godly standards and expectations for their marriages. The boys drank and did not have Christ in their lives. After serious courtship, both of the brothers proposed to the two sisters. One sister told her boyfriend: "You make a choice right now between me and the bottle. I am a believer in Jesus Christ and I will not enter into a marriage with an unbeliever." The guy chose the girl, her Lord, and was saved. The other girl did not ask her boyfriend to make such a choice. She entered into marriage with a alcohol-drinking unbeliever who made her life a living hell.

Every pastor preaches each week to wives worshiping alone without their husbands. I have stood at a church window and observed the number of women who come to church with their children: The mother gets out of the car and the little children fall in behind like chicks following the hen. Where is the father?

Throughout this chapter I am aware there are isolated cases where the husband is a Christian and the wife is not, but these cases are in the decided minority. In most cases the principles here will apply to husbands as well as wives.

How alarmed we are at the divorce statistics—almost 50 percent of marriages ending in divorce. But did you know that divorce between couples of differing faiths occurs three times as often as divorce between members of the same faith? There is a definite risk when one marries an unbeliever or one from another faith. Why do young people take that risk?

Young people feel the thrill of loving and being loved when

they date an unbeliever. These thrills temporarily negate obvious obstacles to a "mixed" marriage. Exciting wedding plans, the beautiful ceremony, and a dream-fulfilled honeymoon temporarily carry the couple along on the assumption that all will be well. They feel (especially the wife) that no problem can be too difficult for them. But saying "I do" doesn't mean you've done it! With the honeymoon over, real life begins, and the problems accompanying a mixed marriage inevitably rear their ugly heads. Soon the believer realizes the pain of what the Bible calls one to be: "unequally yoked." Invariably, the question will be asked: "What should I do when I am married to an unbeliever?"

This important message will be presented in four parts: cases of mixed marriages, causes of mixed marriages, consequences of mixed marriages, and the cure for a mixed marriage.

Cases of Mixed Marriages

Let us identify some mixed marriages found in the Bible and see God's feelings about them.

Abraham's Desire for Isaac

Abraham was growing old and soon would be turning over the leadership to his son, Isaac. There was one important matter weighing on the old patriarch's heart: His son was not married. In Genesis 24, we see the concern of a father for his son's happiness in marriage. Remember the story of how Abraham calls his trusted servant and commissions him to find his son a wife. Not just any woman would do: "thou shalt not take a wife unto my son of the daughter of the Canaanites, among whom I dwell" (v. 3). The women of the Canaanites did not have a personal relationship with Jehovah God. Abraham did not want Isaac yoked to an unbeliever. So, he sent his servant on a great journey to his home country where he knew women who believed in God. We see here the heart of God manifested in Abraham: God does not want us to be unequally yoked! I also personally believe matters of this sort would go smoother if the father of the children were as interested and as involved as Abraham.

Esau's Mixed Marriages

God blessed Isaac's marriage to Rebekah in the birth of twins: Esau and Jacob. The Bible speaks clearly of Esau's disdain for spiritual things. Even though he knew the will of God concerning marriage, Esau "took to wife Judith the daughter of Beeri the Hittite, and Bashemath the daughter of Elon the Hittite" (Gen. 26:34). These were women outside the covenant promise with God. The Bible says they "were a grief of mind unto Isaac and to Rebekah" (v. 35). No doubt, these two wives of Esau neither desired the blessings nor dreaded the curse of God. As unbelieving daughters-in-law, they probably quarreled with Isaac and Rebekah and rebelled against their religious instruction. Esau compounded his spiritual problems by marrying unbelievers. His home would not be a comfort to him.

Moses' Counsel

We again recognize the desire of God concerning marriage when we hear Moses' instructions before the Israelites entered the promised land. In Deuteronomy 7:1-6, we discover that God expressly told the Israelites not to make any form of covenant with the seven pagan nations. God clearly says: "Neither shalt thou make marriages with them; thy daughter thou shalt not give unto his son, nor his daughter shalt thou take unto thy son" (v. 3). Someone may ask: "Really, now, what is the harm in marrying someone who is an unbeliever?"

Let God give His answer to that: "For they will turn away thy son from following me, that they may serve other gods" (v. 4). I honestly believe that I have seen the ungodly influence the godly more than I have the godly influence the ungodly in marriage. God did not want His people to marry unbelievers.

Joshua's Advice

We view evidence of God's desire further communicated by Joshua in Joshua 23:11-13. The faithful old leader urges his people to love God and take heed to themselves by not making marriages with pagan nations. His reason is profound: "they shall be snares and traps unto you, and scourges in your sides, and thorns in your eyes, until ye perish from off this good land which the Lord your God hath given you" (v. 13). Talk to any godly believer who has had the experience of a mixed marriage, and he will say the Bible is true at this point. The unbelieving partner becomes a hindrance, a drawback to the joys and progress in the Christian life. "Snares . . . traps . . . scourges . . . thorns"—most vivid in the way a believer is plagued by a relationship with an unbeliever.

Samson's Mixed Marriages

The strongest man who ever lived could not overcome his desire for passion. Surely Samson had received spiritual instruction from his parents. He persisted, however, in marrying not one but two women of pagan faiths. The first, in Judges 14, shows Samson's disrespect to God's law and the counsel of his parents. He demanded that his parents make the marriage arrangements with the family of a pagan girl. Hear the words of Samson's parents: "Is there never a woman among the daughters of thy brethren or among all thy people, that thou goest to take a wife of the *uncircumcised* Philistines?" (v. 3, author's italics) "Uncircumcised" shows that the Philistines were not in covenant relationship with Jehovah God. Trouble attended that kind of unholy relationship. Shame and death accompanied his marriage to Delilah in Judges 16.

Solomon's Mixed Marriages

The wisest man who ever lived acted so foolishly when it came to marriage! First Kings 11:1 says, Solomon "loved many strange women." These were from nations of which God had said: "Ye shall not go in to them, neither shall they come in unto you." The reason God had forbidden mixed marriages was that "they will turn away your heart after their gods" (v. 2). We read that Solomon had 700 wives and 300 concubines. As a result of this disobedience, notice the process set for us in the Scriptures:

- "His wives turned away his heart" (v. 4).
- "Solomon did evil in the sight of the Lord" (v. 6).
- "And the Lord was angry with Solomon" (v. 9).
- And the Lord said, "I will surely rend the kingdom from thee, and will give it to thy servant" (v. 11).

• "And the Lord stirred up an adversary unto Solomon" (v. 14). The wisest man who ever lived acted foolishly!

Causes of Mixed Marriages

It is interesting to examine the causes of a mixed marriage. We wish we could keep "Humpty-Dumpty" from ever falling off the wall—most of our ministry is helping to put Humpty back together again! The following gives three reasons why mixed marriages happen.

Ignorance

Some mixed marriages are formed because of honest ignorance on behalf of the partners. These people may come from a church where God's Word was not expounded and taught concerning marriage principles. The pastor did not instruct his people in how to find the right mate the first time and how to seek God's will for one's life. The partners had never heard teachings from these passages: 1 Peter 3:1-7; 2 Corinthians 6:14-18; and 1 Corinthians 7 (this chapter has dynamite family/marriage material in it!). As a result, a believer married an unbeliever without any counselor giving warning or wisdom about the situation.

Let me give you a painful, honest confession at this point. My sister married a man who had been married several times before. He was a good man, and we all loved him. However, I did not have any godly convictions at that time concerning the home and finding God's will in marriage. My sister had no one in her immediate family to lovingly and wisely share God's Word to her and give God's counsel. I feel very much an accessory to her painful ten years of marriage and tragic divorce. "My people are destroyed for lack of knowledge" (Hos. 4:6).

Willful Disobedience

Samson married an unbeliever willingly, disregarding the counsel of his parents. Esau also disobeyed God's will as given by his parents. When a believer becomes emotionally involved with someone, it is difficult to turn them to consider God's way. This is why we must have godly convictions before our emotions overcome our reason and will. A girl must not wait to say "no" when she is wrapped in a boyfriend's arms in the seat of a parked car. God says: "Gather me the people together, and I will make them hear my words, that they may learn to fear me all the days that they shall live upon the earth" (Deut. 4:10). Do you see the process? The Word of God is heard in order that fear (respect, honor) for God's way is accepted.

Of course, we have all witnessed the tragic results when two young people willfully disobey clear scriptural guidelines. I remember a young couple who wanted to be married. Both sets of parents were against this union. The boy and girl decided to be married by a judge at the court house. None of the parents were present. This union lasted less than a year before separation and divorce occurred. This happens all too often in the cases of mixed marriages where God and the Scriptures were ignored, where a born-again Christian has willingly disobeyed God's clear-cut commands concerning marriage.

Circumstances

I heard a leader with the Billy Graham Crusade ministry remark that one of the predominant problems after a citywide crusade involved the effects of mixed marriages. The situation would be like this: Two unbelievers marry, live together for several years, have conflict, and divorce. They remarry and start another life and family. Later, the Billy Graham Crusade comes to town and one or both are converted. The next morning they awaken and think: *What am I doing? I have a living mate and/or children somewhere else. Should I go back to them now that I am a Christian*? The Graham team advice is to stay where you are and help your present spouse to become a godly mate.

A pastor encounters this circumstance often in his ministry. The church reaches out with the gospel, and a wife (or husband) is saved. She (he) begins to hear God's Word about life, marriage, and being a godly spouse. Now, the church and the wife (husband) must cooperate in reaching that lost husband (wife).

Characteristics of Mixed Marriages

An Old Testament passage showing vivid principles concerning mixed marriages is Deuteronomy 22:9-11. Notice God giving counsel about "mixed seed" (v. 9). An admonition concerning "mixing animals" (v. 10). Also, there is teaching about "mixed clothing" (v. 11). Imagine trying to plow with an ox yoked with a donkey! There are differences in size, step, and disposition. God also forbade linen and wool mixed together in clothing: Wool was sweat-producing, and as such symbolized sin; linen was clean and represented righteousness.

A New Testament passage illustrating God's principle concerning a mixed marriage is 2 Corinthians 6:14-17. The main theme of this passage is: "Be ye not unequally yoked together with unbelievers" (v. 14). The verb has an imperative aspect to it: Do not try or do not ever incline. The words *unequally yoked* comes from a word *heterozugos*. Notice the part of the word *heteros*, which means different or of another kind. This Scripture goes back to Leviticus 19:19 and Deuteronomy 22:10 where beasts of different kinds were not allowed to be yoked together. The meaning is plain: Believers who had accepted the yoke of Christ, along with grace and reconciliation, are willingly being yoked with unbelievers who have not experienced grace and reconciliation. A cleansed believer with an uncleansed unbeliever—God forbid! A believer, who has faith (*pistis*) joining together with one who is *apistois* (no faith or without faith)—impossible!

Paul punctuates his point of people being together in the Lord by showing the following five contrasts:

- Righteousness cannot fellowship (share with) unrighteousness (v. 14).
- Light has no communion (*koinonia*) with darkness (v. 14).
- Christ has no agreement (symphony—or playing together in harmony) with Belial (devil) (v. 15).
- A believer can have no portion with an unbeliever (v. 15).
- God's sanctuary cannot have idols in it (v. 16).

These contrasts point out a strong "definitely not!" to the question: "Can an unbeliever and a believer be joined together?"

A verse that speaks loudly and clearly to the situation is Amos 3:3, "Can two walk together, except they be agreed?" The following is a list of some definite characteristics of a mixed marriage. I hope the characteristics point out the impossibility of a mixed relationship.

Spiritual Consequences

Please remember that there are three levels to every marriage relationship: (1) sexual—the physical relationship; (2) social—joined in soul and as friends; and (3) spiritual—joined in spirit which is the most intimate part. Can you see how a believer and an unbeliever would be on a different wave length if married? They would not be on the same frequency. In sports terminology "they would be in different leagues!" When you have a believer married to an unbeliever, you have light versus darkness, life versus death, God versus the devil, and heaven versus the earth. There is simply no way this couple can share the spiritual joys and blessings God intended for marriage. They are unable to share worship, prayer, or fellowship together!

The following is what eventually happens to a saved wife (or husband) who is living in a mixed marriage:

- She (he) envies other Christian couples.
- She (he) becomes depressed.
- She (he) becomes impatient with husband's (wife's) progress.
- She (he) becomes unfulfilled in Christian service and worship.
- She (he) eventually becomes totally discouraged and lost to the cause of Christ.

Here is what is going on in an unsaved husband's (wife's) heart and mind: He (she) is ignorant of spiritual matters. As a matter of fact, they are foolishness to him (1 Cor. 2:14). The unsaved husband (wife) begins to become jealous of the Lord and the church, because they are taking so much of his (her) wife's (husband's) time. He (she) may become bitter at the pastor. He (she) feels something or someone has come between him (her) and his (her) wife (husband).

Social Adjustments

Invariably there will be social adjustments to make when a saved person lives with an unsaved mate. There are two main differences that will have to be faced: different friends and different activities. Who do you think the friends of the saved person will be? Christians! And, who do you think the unsaved one will gravitate toward? Unbelievers! Can you imagine the conflict? And, to compound matters, where do you think this couple will go on dates? What if the saved partner has strong convictions about places serving alcohol or that has questionable entertainment? Can you envision the ongoing conflict?

Clashing Loyalties

Both saved and unsaved partners will possess some unbending loyalties. For instance, you know the myriads of activities many alive churches have. Someone has observed that one almost has to be supernatural to keep up with all that happens in many churches! Imagine the saved mate's desires—Sunday School, worship, evening activities, Wednesday prayer service, mission activities, revivals, and the like. How will this set with one's partner's plans? A man informs his wife: "Honey, don't forget next weekend. The company has a golf tournament at the state park. It'll be an all-day affair. We'll take the whole family—golf, swimming, good food. You'll love it!"

The wife goes over to her calendar. "Oh, Sweetheart, I can't go. This is the Saturday before our revival begins. We have a visitation blitz that day." Do you see the clash?

Let me illustrate another definite clash: finances. The saved mate begins to learn about God's plan of economy. That mate feels convicted that they should honor God with the tithe. The other mate is outraged! He (she) doesn't understand God's will. There is a horrendous conflict over money. By the way, I've seen women tithe without their husband's permission—and vice versa (which I do not advise), and the whole family be blessed because of it!

In-Law Problems

When people marry, they marry into other families. There are different customs and conduct often associated with the new families brought into their lives through marriage. Often a mixed marriage can produce a strain on the convictions of the saved partner. One church couple's father gave a banquet each year. People from all over were invited, and alcoholic beverages were served. The son, a Christian, was always invited and asked to pray the blessing. This reached a point where the couple did not feel comfortable in the surroundings of their family. Concern for their children plus Christian convictions produced tremendous unrest about participating. Mixed marriages may bring in-law conflicts to couples.

Child-Rearing

Invariably one of the characteristics of a mixed marriage will center on the rearing of the children. A saved partner soon has godly convictions as to the upbringing of the children. This person sees children as a heritage of the Lord (Ps. 127:3) and to be brought up in the "nurture and admonition of the Lord" (Eph. 6:4). What happens when the example of the father contradicts the teaching of the Word of God? I have heard some saved mothers say: "No influence is better than bad influence."

A little boy said to his father: "Dad, did you go to Sunday School when you were a boy?"

"Yes, Son, I always went to Sunday School," replied the father as he read his paper.

"Well, Dad, I think I'll quit going; it isn't doing me any good either!" stated the little boy.

What happens when the father keeps the cable channel on his television playing adult programs? What happens when the father's beer is in the refrigerator? What should be done when the father's friends come over and filthy language is freely used? The way the children are reared will certainly be a source of disagreement between saved and unsaved marriage partners. Here I speak not only of fathers but mothers!

The Cure for Mixed Marriages

How our hearts grieve for those unfulfilled marriages where both partners are not saved. We long to impart the truth from God's Word to them that will enable them to win their mate and have a godly home. Our goal should never be anything less than to have a godly home. *Even though most of the following refers to the saved wife, most of these biblical principles can also apply to the saved husband. The Word of God has admonitions for both born-again husbands and wives.*

Notice 1 Peter 3:1-7. In this passage, the ideal woman is mentioned in six verses, and the ideal man can be found in one verse. Peter gives a situation in verse one that is as up-to-date as tomorrow's newspaper: A saved wife is living with a man who does not "obey *the* word" (author's italics). In other words, the husband has not accepted the gospel. Let's notice three principles about how the saved wife can win the unsaved man.

Her Position

The saved wife is told to be in "subjection" to her husband (v. 1). This word *hupotassomenoi* is a military word, and it means to voluntarily rank oneself under the authority of another. An employee voluntarily ranks oneself under the authority of an employer. A student voluntarily ranks oneself under the authority of a teacher. A private in the army voluntarily ranks oneself under the authority of the supervising officer. In all of these cases, those in subjection may be more intelligent, have more energy, and possess a more appealing personality, but they voluntarily rank themselves beneath their appointed superiors.

The wife must be in submission to her husband, if she is to have a Christian home. She may have more intelligence, energy, and personality, but she is to rank herself below her husband. How is she able to do this? "Wives, submit yourselves unto your own husbands, as unto the *Lord*" (Eph. 5:22, author's italics). She submits first to the Lord in her heart and then to her husband.

Is your position with your unsaved husband one of defiance and bitterness? If so, then he will not see Jesus in you. Accept and model the position of subjection. You concentrate on putting Jesus first in your life. Let your ways please Him (Prov. 16:7), and God will change your husband through you.

Her Personality

The wife is to adorn her life with a "meek and quiet spirit" (1 Pet. 3:4). If you try to catch and maintain your husband's attention through the physical (v. 3), you will lose in the end. The flesh and physical fade but the spiritual beauty is incorruptible (v. 4). God's woman is "quiet." She has a tranquil and peaceful spirit. She is inwardly beautiful and has learned to walk with God.

The woman who will win her unsaved husband must major on internal beauty. Her desire is for Christ to be formed in her (Gal. 4:9). She abides in Christ (John 15:4), and the fruit of the Spirit (Gal. 5:22-23) becomes her godly conduct.

Her Performance

Notice in verse 6 that the saved woman is like Sarah as she obeyed and served her husband, Abraham. The wife's conduct and service can be likened to the conduct of the virtuous woman in Proverbs 31:10-31. Verse 5 says the holy women, whom God blessed, "trusted in God." This means to walk by faith. The following list gives some practical aspects of walking by faith in order to win an unsaved mate:

(1) Pray for your husband daily.

(2) Have as many people as you can pray for him—your Sunday School class, godly friends, and relatives.

(3) Stay strong spiritually yourself. You must not allow yourself to backslide or lose your spiritual strength. When you lose your Christlike life, both of you are sunk! Please note: The battle to win your husband may take some time. This means you cannot lose heart or give up. Read your Bible every day and maintain your daily quiet time (Eph. 6:10).

(4) Think positive as based on the Scripture. Read Philippians 4:8. Put those concepts in your mind: truth, honesty, justice, purity, loveliness, good report. Don't allow yourself to be angry and bitter. Beauty comes from meekness and quietness.

(5) Be a great wife! Oftentimes the hardest time of the day is the time frame just before he comes home. Pray during that time. Ask God to help you meet him with joy and love in the Lord. Cook his favorite foods! Clear the night so you can be with him. Minister to your husband. Make him the king of the home. Then, you'll be the queen!

(6) Involve other people in his life. Talk confidentially to your pastor and other godly people about your husband. Invite them to drop by and meet him. Be coy in a spiritual sort of way!

(7) Talk positively about the Lord and the church. Don't nag (1 Pet. 3:1—"the word"). Ask God to give you the right words and spirit as you testify of God's work in your heart. Salt your hus-

band and make him thirsty by keeping him aware of exciting happenings at church. Invite him to musicals, films, special studies, revivals, and fellowships. Eventually, he will come, hear the Word of God, feel His Spirit, and be saved. Really!

A converted Hindu woman was asked by a friend how she was able to live with her unsaved husband. "What do you do when he is angry and persecutes you?"

She replied, "I just cook the food better and sweep the floor a little cleaner."

"How are you able to take it when he speaks unkindly?" her friend asked.

The new creature in Christ responded, "I answer him mildly, trying to show him in every way that, when I became a Christian, I became a better wife."

When a man lives with a sermon, talks with a sermon, sleeps with a sermon, and sees a sermon, he will be won to Christ!

Likewise, a saved husband should live out the gospel before his unsaved spouse. Husbands should love their wives as Christ has loved His church. As Christ died for the church and shed His blood, so should the godly husband be willing to give his life for his wife and children.

The unsaved wife is quite likely to accept the Lord Jesus Christ if she sees the Christ reflected in the life of her own husband.

8

What Should I Do When . . . I Doubt My Salvation?

The young mother called and asked if my wife and I could come see her. She sounded disturbed, so we arrived there as soon as possible. "I have doubts about my salvation," she confided. "Here I am—a mother with children depending on me, and I don't know for sure that I'm going to heaven." As we talked, this mother related how, as a little girl, she walked forward during a service. The pastor asked her if she believed in Jesus, filled out a card on her, and presented her to the church. That turned out to be the extent of her "Christian experience." After talking further with her, all of us fell on our knees, and this woman prayed to receive Jesus Christ as her Savior.

A deacon, who was a pillar of the church for many years, shocked the congregation one evening. He surrendered his deacon ordination papers and related how he had carried a burden for years about his Christian experience. It seems that he simply "joined the church" as a child but truly found the Lord during a revival while in college. Now, the deacon testified, he wanted to put his Christian baptism "in proper order."

The evangelist preached a strong message on the second coming and urged the people to be prepared. For several weeks afterward, the pastor had appointments with members having the same question: "What should I do when I doubt my salvation?" This pastor was faithful in counseling with his members. Some were lost and prayed to receive Christ. Most were already saved but needed counsel concerning their doubts.

One of the predominantly asked questions of pastors throughout the years has been: "What should I do when I doubt my salvation?" A person would be amazed as to the number of "outstanding" and active members who have pondered and posed this question. Many Christians have agonized for years about the validity and security of their salvation experience. Often this is a very private and painful time, because they are embarrassed to admit their doubts.

God wants us to have assurance concerning our salvation! "These things have I written unto you that believe on the name of the Son of God; that ye may *know* that ye *have* eternal life, and that ye may believe on the name of the Son of God" (1 John 5:13, author's italics). God wants us to know and be certain of our relationship to Him. Paul said, "I *know* whom I have believed" (2 Tim. 1:12, author's italics). God's desire is that we go forward and upward for Him. If we have doubts, let us deal with them honestly and from the Scripture.

For this timely topic, let us divide the presentation into the following parts: characteristics of doubt, causes of doubt, and cure for doubt. There could possibly be some painful surprises as we examine this subject. Have our pastors and churches presented the gospel clearly and biblically? Have our churches followed up on our new converts to encourage and instruct them as they begin their walk with the Lord? Do we take seriously our spiritual role as our "brother's keeper"? These and other questions may surface during our study on the Christian and doubt.

Characteristics of Doubt

Doubt means to be uncertain in opinion or belief. When one doubts, one has a mistrust, a suspicion, or a lack of confidence in a certain person, principle, or position.

Doubt in the Bible comes from the verb *aporeo* and the noun *aporia*. This word is made up of two parts: *a* meaning without, and *poros* meaning a way, transit, or resource. *Doubt*, then, would mean without a way or having no solution. One would be at his or her wit's end without resources and at a loss on how to proceed. Sometimes the word *doubt* may be translated as perplexed or in distress.

One of the most vivid illustrations of how doubt happens is found in Matthew 14:22-33. The disciples were sent to the other side of the sea without Jesus. A storm arose at sea, and the disciples were being tossed and turned. In an unforgettable moment, they saw Jesus walking on the water. Peter asked and received permission from Jesus to walk on the water. Miraculously, Peter did walk on the water until he looked at the boisterous waves and then began to sink. Jesus rescued him and then rebuked him by saying, "O thou of little faith, wherefore didst thou *doubt*?" (v. 31, author's italics). It is apparent that Peter's doubts came as he removed his eyes from Jesus and considered only the danger of the elements.

Probably the person in the Bible most associated with doubt is Thomas, a disciple of Jesus. Most people remember these words of Thomas and label him a "doubter": "Except I shall see in his hands the print of the nails, and put my finger into the print of the nails, and thrust my hand into his side, I *will not believe*" (John 20:25, author's italics). We forget, however, that it was Thomas who fearlessly exhorted his fellow disciples: "Let us also go, that we may die with him" (John 11:16). And we are so indebted to Thomas for interrupting our Lord's discourse on heaven by imploring, "Lord, we know not whither thou goest; and how can we know the way?" (John 14:5). This was not a doubter but a seeker after truth. At the end, however, we see Thomas and all who desire truth at the same place—at Jesus' feet, confessing Him as Lord and God. If you ever have doubts, God will meet those doubts with loving proof and assurance. The natural inclination will be to bow and worship.

Causes of Doubt

Why do people doubt their salvation and security in Christ? Some of these answers may be obvious, while others you may not have considered. Also, the cure for doubt will be interwoven into the description of the causes. If you have ever doubted, I hope you will be helped by the diagnosis of the causes.

Lack of Understanding About Salvation

Over the years, I have talked with fellow pastors about doubt. The consensus among my colleagues is that most people who come to us about doubt were genuinely saved. However, they were never discipled and instructed as to the total nature of their salvation.

Paul gives a capsule statement of our salvation's nature in Ephesians 1:13-14:

- After you heard the word of truth, you were saved.
- After you were saved, you were sealed with the Holy Spirit of promise.
- The Holy Spirit is the earnest, the guarantee of our inheritance in glory.
- The Holy Spirit will keep us sealed until God personally redeems His purchased possession.

A man saved his money and took his wife on a picturesque cruise. The weather was perfect, and the couple enjoyed seeing the magnificent ocean and the quaint and exotic ports. However, the couple was never seen at mealtimes: They were on deck or in their cabin. Further research revealed that they were eating cheese and crackers, snacks, and fruit brought from home. They did not realize that the payment of their fare also included three great meals each day, plus several delicious brunches and buffets!

Many Christians are eating cheese and crackers and are unaware God's salvation "package" includes "all things that pertain unto life and godliness" (2 Pet. 1:3). Ignorance reigns in the minds and hearts of most Christians concerning the nature and extent of their wonderful salvation.

Did you know that, when you receive Christ:

- You can *never perish* and no man (or anything or anyone else) can pluck you out of Jesus' hand (John 10:28)? *Perish* does not refer to physical life, but eternal, spiritual life. Read and meditate on this verse!
- You have Jesus' relationship and companionship *always* (Matt. 28:20)?
- You possess the Holy Spirit *forever* (John 14:16)?
- Nothing can separate you from the love of God (Rom. 8:38-39)?

These and many more Scriptures illustrate to us God's magnificent relationship with us that keeps us saved and safe. In my short lifetime of ministry, I humbly suggest to you that most of the people (including ministers!) who doubted "once saved, always saved" may have had a *suspect doctrine* of salvation. Quite often one who denies the precious keeping ability and ministry of God has a doctrine of salvation based on works. I find the following true that some:

- Believe you are saved by works and kept by works. To which I reply, "for by the works of the law shall no flesh be justified" (Gal. 2:16).
- Believe you are saved by grace and faith but kept by works. To which I reply, "Are ye so foolish? having begun in the Spirit, are ye now made perfect by the flesh?" (Gal. 3:3).
- Believe you are saved by grace and faith and kept by God's grace alone. To which I refer, "For by grace are ye saved through faith; and that not of yourselves: it is the gift of God: Not of works, lest any man should boast" (Eph. 2:8-9).

The ability to believe and make contact with God is a gift from God. Salvation, from start to finish, is of grace in order that it be of God, not humans.

I am taking more time on this first cause of doubt than any of the others because the lack of understanding underlies more doubt than any other cause. "Ye do err, not knowing the scriptures, nor the power of God" (Matt. 22:29). "My people are destroyed for lack of knowledge" (Hos. 4:6). Most Christians do not know and appreciate the provisions and protections God has "inbuilt" with their salvation! Read John 3:16 again. What does this verse say? It does say:

- whosoever *believeth* in him (trust, rely on, cling to),
- should *not perish* (die spiritually or ever be separated from the life and love of God),
- but *have* everlasting life (*Have* means to possess.),
- but have *everlasting life* (How long is "everlasting"? Is it forever? Do you see any conditions on this everlasting life except "believe?").

Please take God at His Word! God is faithful and just (1 John 1:9). What He has said He will do in your life when you trust Jesus: He has done! Walk by faith in His Word (2 Cor. 5:7).

Unconfessed Sin

Possibly the second most common cause for doubt is unconfessed sin. Christians do sin after salvation, because they are not yet in their perfect bodies and in their perfect home in glory. Even after salvation, we must face three great challenges: the world, the flesh, and the devil. The penalty of sin was dealt with by justification. The presence of sin will one day be dealt with by glorification. The power of sin which we face daily in this life is dealt with by our sanctification. Christians do sin and must deal with it properly.

A Soviet archaeological expedition in Egypt was given a mummy. The mummy was sent back home for study, and the first order of business was to determine its age. The scientists, however, were pushed aside by the secret police who said, "Leave it to us; we will find out." Presently the secret police announced that the mummy's age was 4,840 years.

"Amazing," cried the Soviet scientists. "How did you determine it?"

"Easy," said the secret police. "The mummy confessed."

No one is going to make you confess your sins—but you better be honest with God every day! We all have sins of commission, omission, and disposition. "If we say that we have no sin, we deceive ourselves, and the truth is not in us" (1 John 1:8). Sin is like ashes which eventually cover the fire. When we confess that God "is faithful and just to forgive us our sins, and to cleanse us from all unrighteousness" (v.9), there is a joy in being forgiven and cleansed. "Blessed are they whose iniquities are forgiven, and whose sins are covered" (Rom. 4:7). Being forgiven results in happiness, joy, cleansing, and open channels to God and man.

There is a vicious cycle operating in the Christian's life, if one does not confess one's sins to God. Eventually, we have a horrible guilt that covers us. We feel separated from God, especially in our prayer life. Because we are not walking in the light, we are unable to have fellowship with our family of faith (1 John 1:7). God seems farther and farther away. We may come to a point of denying God's existence and His relationship with us. I have known people whose lives were miserable, because they were carrying around unconfessed sin and unresolved conflict. Unconfessed sin can make you doubt the validity of your relationship with God.

Spiritual Inactivity

I have seen people doubt their relationship with God because they became "rusty" in their spiritual service. A couple came into our area from another state. They had been Sunday School teachers, choir members, and workers in the bus ministry. The new area and church intimidated them. They thought they would "rest" a while and then volunteer when the new year began in October. However, days became months, and months became years. By the time I visited them, they were so miserable, even to the point of doubting if what they had felt and done earlier was real.

I believe inactivity caused John the Baptist to doubt. Remember that John was put in prison, and he sent a message to Jesus: "Art thou he that should come, or do we look for another?" (Matt. 11:3). Remember that this is the man who pointed Jesus out by saying: "Behold the Lamb of God, which taketh away the sin of the world" (John 1:29). I believe inactivity in prison caused John to doubt if Jesus was the Messiah.

The Christian is happiest when serving the Lord. We are to be "doers of the word, and not hearers only, deceiving your own selves" (Jas. 1:22). When we are serving faithfully, we are in the Word, in prayer, and in fellowship with God and man.

Unrealistic Expectations

Some people have doubted because the Christian life turned out to be different than they were led to believe. Some actually felt all their troubles would go away, and they would never experience opposition again! Others felt that their lives would be in a constant state of heavenly happiness with God taking care of all their problems.

Of course, the joy of conversion is unforgettable, and our lives should be lived in power and happiness. But, it's sort of like marriage: Saying "I do" doesn't mean we've done it! At salvation, God comes into our lives and equips us to live victoriously for Him. But, that doesn't mean we won't be tempted and tried. "The trying of your faith worketh patience" (Jas. 1:3). "Blessed is the man that endureth temptation" (v. 12). God has a purpose for our trials. We grow through overcoming the problems and obstacles which cross our life's path.

All of us love "mountaintop" living! What a joy it was to be with Jesus on the mount of transfiguration. It felt so good that Peter wanted to stay there (Matt. 17:4). Remember Jesus dealt with the demon-possessed boy. Peter, upon seeing that boy foaming at the mouth and wallowing in the fire, probably wished he was back on the mountain! We will have our mountaintop experiences, and they will equip us to minister in the valleys. Some people, however, feel that God is nowhere around if they don't have goosebumps an inch high!

Understand the nuts and bolts of the Christian life. We will have problems, but see problems as opportunities in disguise. God filters every experience that comes to us, and there is a purpose behind every trial (Rom. 8:28).

Comparing Others

When I was in seminary, I had an older pastor preach a revival for me. I came to know this dear man well that week. He was close to the Lord. He was seemingly in control of his emotions, thoughts, and desires—so much so that I felt inferior to him! When that week was over, I almost thought I was not saved. I was comparing myself to another person.

Has this ever happened to you? Have you ever compared yourself to another Christian and felt like: "I don't have what that person has! I must not be saved!"

Occasionally, we will have evangelists who have marvelous, "Hollywood-type" testimonies. Their lives before Christ were so wicked, hellish, and vivid in sin—then, Christ made such a dramatic change in their lives! Here's a person in our church listening to this, and they compare their quiet, gentle conversion to a former gang leader or drug user. They don't realize it took as much grace to save a good but lost person as it did a wild drunkard.

Don't compare yourself with other people. God spoke to you on your wavelength and met you at your point of need. You answered His call by repenting, believing, and calling upon His name. Now you should concentrate on growing in grace and knowing of Him (2 Pet. 3:18).

Cure for Doubt

You may have already sensed a premise of mine: I believe that most people who doubt are saved. To me, doubt is a sign of life, not death! Dead people do not doubt. Why would Satan stir up a person who is "dead in trespasses and in sin?" (Eph. 2:1). That is when God "quickens" a person. In my small and short ministry, I have found that most doubting people genuinely trusted Christ with their whole heart the first time. Then, possibly, they:

- were not instructed in the Christian life,
- lacked understanding in the nature and extent of salvation,
- let unconfessed sin build up in their lives,
- had unrealistic expectations of the Christian life,
- compared themselves to a "super Christian."

I heard a speaker liken doubt to pain. Where there is no pain, there is a lack of feeling and death. Where there is life, there will be pain. For example, as you trim your nails, you cut away the dead parts. Upon reaching the "live" part, you get into the "quick" and feel pain because there is life! Doubt is a sign of life, not death.

Passage Study

As a prelude to some practical suggestions of cure, I want to examine Hebrews 6:4-6. Notice these points:

Five characteristics of a saved person are given. The key here is that they are expressed in aorist principles. This refers to a point in the past which cannot be relived over again. The tense of "once-for-all" governs these participles describing five characteristics of a saved person.

"Once enlightened" (v. 4).—This means they received a revelation. The darkness was removed and they "saw the light." This revelation is a natural way to describe a conversion experience and is the certain work of the Holy Spirit. The tense of "once-for-all" qualifies and governs the participle.

"Tasted of the heavenly gift" (v. 4).—Not only were they enlightened, but they "tasted" or experienced the heavenly gift.

Usually, the *gift* refers to Jesus and/or eternal life (Rom. 6:23; John 4:10). To *taste* means to be stirred in heart and to experience spiritual reality. Jesus "tasted" death for every man (see Heb. 2:9)—this doesn't mean He just sampled death and spat it out: He drank the whole cup! I emphasize again that, when the Scripture says they "tasted," it cannot be repeated: a once-for-all time.

"Made [partners] of the Holy Ghost" (v. 4).—The word for *partner* (partaker—KJV) means associate, colleague, or companion. *Partner* refers to one who participates with another in a common activity or possession. This term, describing the Christian experience, shows the relationship with Holy Spirit. From now on, the Holy Spirit is not a stranger or an enemy but a partner! This word is found in other passages (Luke 5:7; Hebrews 1:9; 3:1,14). The tense is aorist and is a never to be repeated experience for those participating.

"Tasted the good word of God" (v. 5).—The believer has experienced fully the enjoyment of God's Word. He can say from personal experience that God is true to His Word and faithful to His promises. This, we emphasize, is a "once-for-all" participle. The believer has proven that God is true to His Word.

"Tasted . . . the powers of the world to come" (v. 5).—*Taste,* we believe, means to experience fully. *Powers* refers to miracles and mighty works. Since being saved, the believer has experienced the fruit of a changed life. These mighty happenings are a foretaste of a millennial age—the heavenly age has become a reality in one's life! This could refer to healings, habits broken, prayers answered, people saved and other mighty results of being saved. This participle, also, is aorist and implies a one time happening with the results still coming.

The writer could not have chosen expressions which more forcefully describe the possession of a real and genuine Christian life. These five characteristics are given as actual spiritual experiences. They are verifiable in our own experience, are they not?

The issue in Hebrews 6:4-6 is not whether a person can be lost after being saved. The issue is: Can a person ever be saved again if he or she loses his or her original salvation? In other words, after a human is spiritually enlightened, tastes the heavenly gift, becomes a partaker of the Holy Ghost, tastes the good Word of God, and tastes the powers of the world to come if one can lose the effects of that, can a person ever be saved again? The answer is *"no!"* If a person can lose one's wonderful salvation, which is purchased by Jesus' death on the cross, that person can never be saved again. If Jesus' death and resurrection were not powerful enough to keep a person saved the first time, what good would a repeat salvation be? Jesus' salvation work would be shamed and disgraced (v. 6). To be saved again would require a second work of Christ in death and resurrection: This will never happen again (Rom. 6:10).

Have you experienced the five characteristics of the saved person as found in Hebrews 6:4-5? If so, then salvation has become effective throughout the remainder of time and eternity. The effects of salvation are irreversible. To be saved and lose our salvation is to say: "My sin is stronger than the power of the cross and the resurrection." Christ's salvation work happened once and for all. We become God's children and certain for heaven when we: (1) Repent—Luke 13:3 and (2) believe upon Christ and call upon His name—Romans 10:9,10,13. If we could "fall away" (Heb. 6:6), it would be impossible (v. 4) to be renewed again unto repentance (v. 6). Christ's first payment is disgraced if we think His redemption work cannot save us eternally. There is no hope of salvation the second time, because there will never be another crucifixion and resurrection.

Practical Suggestions

Ask God to help you recall the happenings of your profession of faith.—Paul reminisced about the faith of Timothy's family (2 Tim. 1:5). Did you experience conviction about your need for Christ? Did you pray and ask Jesus to come into your life? I have dealt with some who received assurance and peace only after they made a definite commitment which they could remember. I do not want to make you doubt, but if uncertainty persists, "drive down a definite stake" now by praying and committing to Christ.

Claim the Word of God.—Take your Bible and read all the verses dealing with *saved, salvation, faith,* and *believe.* Remember: "Faith cometh by hearing, and hearing by the word of God"

(Rom. 10:17). Take God at His Word and walk by it.

Differentiate between faith, fact, and feeling.—So many govern the validity of their experience by feelings. What are the facts of God's Word? Put your faith in the facts. Then, there may or may not be feelings. Do not let feelings and emotions govern your life! You are not saved by feelings or kept by feelings.

Confess all sin.—You may have a besetting sin which continues to plague you. Claim 1 John 1:9. Ask God to reveal to you any hidden parts of your heart harboring disobedience. Cooperate with God in cleaning guilt, bitterness, and ill-will to any brother—clear away the ashes so the bells of joy can ring!

Be active in service.—Let God lead you to the place of service and be faithful in serving God. The happiest people are active people. Talk to your pastor about where you should serve.

Be a thankful person.—Be thankful. A rejoicing person will not be moody or a slave to "stinking" thinking (Phil. 4:4). Express your praise to God daily (1 Thess. 5:16).

There was once an Irish boy gravely ill in the hospital. A Christian nurse shared the plan of salvation with him. However, his background could not go past the sacraments, penance, and confessionals. The nurse left a New Testament with him and urged him to pray and study certain passages on salvation. A week passed before she was on duty again. When she saw him, the first thing she noticed was his shining face. "I always knew Jesus was necessary," the newly saved boy said. "But I never knew until yesterday that He was enough!"

Jesus is enough! Tell Him your doubts. Listen for His voice through your Bible study, prayer time, and worship experiences. With all my heart I believe you, like Thomas, will soon be at His feet crying out, "My Lord and my God" (John 20:28).

9

What Should I Do When . . . My Mate Asks Me for a Divorce?

Connie radiated that indescribable glow of all brides throughout time as she came down the aisle in her antique-white lace gown. Steve, her groom, trying not to seem too silly in the only tuxedo he had ever worn, was happy, too. And when the minister intoned, "You may kiss the bride," both felt that rush of pleasure and fear reserved for great events. They were in love, and now they were married. More than 90 percent of all Americans marry, and most feel that surge of love.

Five years later, Connie and Steve sat in a lawyer's office. In rage, agony, and sorrow, a divorce was being negotiated. "I thought we were in love," says Connie, "and we were. But after we married, he hardly said, 'I love you.' "

"She may have thought she was in love," says Steve. "But she never did anything I wanted—in or out of bed."

A famous golfer was sued for divorce by his wife of nine years. His wife cited a conflict of personalities and said the relationship had become insupportable because of discord. Both felt there was no expectation of reconciliation.

A newspaper carried the major article, "Runaway Wives: What Makes Them Run?" The article described the rash of women and mothers who have left their husbands and children. The number of one-parent homes, headed by the father, has risen dramatically in the last twenty years. The article reported that the main reason women leave home was because they feel unrecognized and unappreciated.

Outside of death, the breakup of a home has the most traumatic effects upon one's life. It is a devastating shock when a spouse is asked for a divorce by his or her mate. I remember 1963 as well as yesterday when I came home from baseball practice and found my mother crying. My father had come back home during the morning, packed his clothes, and had moved to another city. My mother was notified she was being sued for divorce. That experience between my mother and father has dramatically affected me, my wife, and my children since that time. Taken individually, I have never met a man finer than my father or a woman more wonderful than my mother: They somehow could not keep the marriage together.

A woman was once asked why she had never married. "Why should I?" she replied. "I've got a parrot that cusses, a dog that snores, a chimney that smokes, and a cat that doesn't come home at night! Why do I want a husband?" The truth is that most people will marry. We need to work to make our marriages as happy and sound as possible. The key is to find the right person the first time!

This chapter is organized into three sections: the covenant of marriage, causes of divorce, and the cure for divorce. As a pastor, I am particularly disturbed at two happenings within family crises: the rise of divorce among Christian families and the increasing number of wives leaving their husbands and children. I am not surprised that a book has come out on *How to Do Your Own Divorce*—without the help of lawyers. The book has the proper forms and instructions. It has become a best-seller!

The Covenant of Marriage

A man purchased a swing set for his little boy. Of course, the swing had to be assembled and the man, an engineer by profession, plunged into the task. Soon he had a weird contortion of bars and poles going nowhere and doing nothing! Very humbly, the engineer father decided to consult the instruction manual. Soon the little boy was enjoying the swing.

Everyone agrees that something is wrong with the American home. Over recent years, however, it's been like the weather: No one can do anything about it! Some people have given up on the home. A Hollywood actress has said publicly several times that it is almost unnatural for two people to live together for the rest of their lives. I submit that America has forsaken the instruction manual—the Bible! When in doubt, read the instructions!

Just as God is the Designer and Architect of creation, He has a plan for the home. When God's plan for the home is followed, the home will be successful. God is not the author of confusion, but of peace (1 Cor. 14:33). Notice God's fourfold plan for the home:

Partnership

As God completed His creation, He saw all the animals enjoying their partners. And God said, "It is not good that the man should be alone." The loneliness and incompleteness of man brought about a "help meet for him" (Gen. 2:18). God specially created one that would be bone of his bones and flesh of his flesh (v. 23). The miracle of marriage brings two people out of their present relationship into a new union where they are "one flesh" (v. 24).

Man was meant to have a partner, a companion. I have seen two people love each other so much and live together so long they look alike! (Sometimes even their dog looks like them!). Marriage brings two people so close that, when one cries, the other tastes salt. Our associate pastor and his wife have a gorgeous marriage which has lasted over fifty years. They are very close! One day Mrs. Lasater was having surgery. I went to the hospital to pray with them and arrived after the nurse had given her a "knockout" shot. When I came through the door Brother Lasater was holding her hand, and he was asleep, not her! They are so close. The first plan for God's home is partnership.

Propagation

A second reason for marriage is the propagation of the human race. The only plan God has to populate the earth is the Christian family. God said, "Be fruitful, and multiply, and replenish the earth" (Gen. 1:28). People violate God's plan when children are born out of wedlock and without the confines of a Christian marriage. "Children are an heritage of the Lord: and the fruit of the womb is his reward" (Ps. 127:3). God needs the home for propagation.

Purity

God's third plan for the home involves the way people are to meet their great need for intimacy. "To avoid fornication, let every man have his own wife, and let every woman have her own husband" (1 Cor. 7:2). The only way humans are to meet their God-given need for sex is through Christian marriage. "Marriage is honorable in all, and the bed undefiled: but whoremongers and adulterers God will judge" (Heb. 13:4). Sex before marriage is sin, and people are to be faithful to their mates after marriage. Marriage is God's way to meet a person's need for sex.

Picture

When we see a happy home, we see a picture of heaven on earth (Ps. 128). The husband's relationship to his wife symbolizes Christ's relationship to the church. The wife's relationship to her husband pictures the church's relationship to Christ. "Husbands, love your wives, even as Christ also loved the church, and gave himself for it" (Eph. 5:25). People of earth should be reminded of the church and heaven when a godly home functions properly before their eyes. God's relationship to Israel and Christ's relationship to the church are pictured as two people joining their lives together.

Above all descriptions, marriage is likened to a "covenant." Today we are seeing an increase in marriage "contracts": The man and woman sign premarriage agreements as to the disposition of material belongings in case of divorce. However, marriage in God's eyes is a covenant, not a business contract. Two people die to self and become one in the Lord. A relationship happens which is indissoluble: One cannot be divided! When you research *covenant* in the Bible, you will find such a binding agreement that only death can break. In Christian marriage, vows are made that are binding which add solemnity and sanctity to the covenant (Eccl. 5:2-6; Ps. 50:14; 66:13; Isa. 19:21).

How God's heart is broken by the violence upon the marriage covenant today! He hates divorce (Mal. 2:16), but not the divorcees. God is the unseen Witness at every marriage, and He grieves when man severs the bond between his companion and wife of his covenant (v.14). I wish America would see marriage as two people entering into covenant with God and each other for the rest of their lives.

Causes of Divorce

The typical American home, composed of a husband, wife, and children, is almost an extinct species today. Why would a man ask his wife for a divorce? Before I share the main ways I have seen divorce come to a home, let me list what the law says. On the law books in the state of Tennessee, there are fourteen ways a person can obtain a divorce. These are found in "Tennessee Codes Annotated" (1988) and are the Tennessee causes of divorce from the bonds of matrimony:

(1) That either party, at the time of contract, was and still is naturally impotent and incapable of procreation;

(2) That either party has knowingly entered into a second marriage, in violation of a previous marriage, still subsisting;

(3) That either party has committed adultery;

(4) Willful or malicious desertion or absence of either party, without a reasonable cause, for one (1) whole year;

(5) Being convicted of any crime which, by the laws of the state, renders the party infamous;

(6) Being convicted of a crime which, by the laws of the state, is declared to be a felony, and sentenced to confinement in the penitentiary;

(7) That either party has attempted the life of the other, by poison or any other means showing malice;

(8) Refusal, on the part of a wife or husband, to remove with his or her spouse to this state, without a reasonable cause, and willfully absenting himself from the spouse residing in Tennessee for two (2) years;

(9) That the woman was pregnant at the time of the marriage, by another person, without the knowledge of the husband;

(10) Habitual drunkenness or abuse of narcotic drugs of either party, when the husband or wife has contracted either such habit after marriage;

(11) Irreconcilable differences between the parties;

(12) That the husband or wife is guilty of such cruel and inhu-

man treatment or conduct towards the spouse as renders cohabitation unsafe and improper;

(13) That the husband has offered such indignities to the wife's person as to render her condition intolerable, and thereby forced her to withdraw;

(14) That he has abandoned her, or turned her out of doors, and refused or neglected to provide for her.

There are fourteen causes of marriage breakup in my state. Do you know something? Not a one of them is scriptural! In the eyes of almighty and all-loving God, not a one of them is scriptural grounds for severing a marriage relationship!

Why would a mate ask a spouse for a divorce? Let me name the most frequent causes for divorce.

Lack of Faith

The most dangerous relationship is that of a Christian to a non-Christian in marriage. This is called a "mixed" marriage or being unequally yoked. A Christian faces a difficult path in a bond with one whose loyalty is not to Jesus Christ. There will be different friends, activities, and sympathies. Usually in this situation, the unbelieving mate seeks the divorce. Satan controls and twists his mind and persuades him to leave his only sanctifying relationship (1 Cor. 7:14).

Adultery

What a fiery dart of Satan adultery is today! Satan has America inflamed with perverted passion. Sex sells products of all kinds. Nudity invades our homes regularly through television and home movies. Scandalous divorce among visible politicians, entertainers, and Christians has weakened the church's stand for morality and the Christian home. The extremes of the women's movement have produced an aggressive female who cannot be handled spiritually by America's male. We see surveys often showing the shocking occurrence of affairs among working people. Very few marriage partners can forgive, forget, and restore when adultery invades a home.

Money Problems

Many experts deem this the number one problem in America's homes. The average American home spent 110 percent of its income last year. The credit card trap, impulsive shopping, and mismanagement are the culprits of debt. There are few gut-wrenchers worse than having bill collectors hounding you all the time! Sometimes a person must work two jobs to maintain a standard of living. This means physical fatigue, poor communication, and lack of quality time. Working mothers seldom make enough to compensate for child care, car costs and maintenance, clothing, insurance, food (office and home), and quality time given to the job instead of the family. The Bible is still true: "the love of money is the root of all evil: which while some coveted after, they have *erred from the faith*, and *pierced themselves* through with *many sorrows* (1 Tim. 6:10, author's italics). When a Christian begins to worship money, he or she follows the same painful process that an unsaved person follows. Financial pressure and greed turn a mate's heart.

Unthoughtfulness

Courtship should never end! Remember how courteous and kind we were before marriage? Over the years, however, we begin to take one another for granted. Ingratitude and discourtesy set in while affection and attention disappear. We reach a stage that when someone else shows attention that a schoolboy or schoolgirl infatuation happens! A man may begin to think he really doesn't love his wife any more. Listen! We must keep the love fresh by kindness, loving surprises, gifts, phone calls, and, especially, staying in love with Jesus. Do you pray together?

Preoccupation

Life is so busy. There are so many schedules and deadlines. We have runaway fathers and absentee mothers who are producing latch-key children. A high percentage of children under five have single-parent homes. Our children are being reared by baby-sitters, day care, teachers, coaches, and the television. A man centers his life around his job. A wife feels this rejection and begins to center her life around her children and home. The home becomes a motel, restaurant, and a filling station. Do you know how to spell *love*? T-I-M-E! Relationships must have time to be nourished. Schedule time with your mate!

In the counseling I have done over the years, these five causes are the most predominant. We could have mentioned in-law problems, poor appearance, addictive habits, and poor communication. Poor communication eventually enters the situation, whatever the problem. I am so thankful my wife has literally forced me to talk about problems over the years. A male will do practically anything to keep from talking to his wife about their problems! Many times over the years, however, Marilynn has said, "OK, big boy, we've got to talk." We have *always* been able to settle our problems.

I am a better man today because of my wife's tears. Again, most men do not like to be around a crying woman (mother, sister, girlfriend, wife, or secretary!). My wife is not a crybaby and has not cried that much in over twenty years of marriage. But, when she has cried, it has been effective! For my wife to cry, it means she is overloaded or doing something she is not equipped to do. A wife crying is like an overloaded fuse! I realize I am not fulfilling my husband or father role when she cries, and this has made me improve over the years. I have done a lot more changing in our marriage relationship than my wife! Of course, I had more to change.

A final note about causes—problems do not develop overnight. Occasionally, a pastor might have a situation where the husband or wife inherited a drug problem from the beginning. However, a relationship deteriorates over the years from the inside. "Termites" can be destroying a home, and the occupants are not even aware of it. Stealthily and insidiously the little creatures are eating away at the very foundations without the owners' knowledge. One of my family's favorite vacation places is St. Augustine, Florida. We always visit the Old Fort. Did you know the Old Fort, which has never been defeated, is losing in a battle with algae? We were told that the materials of the Old Fort with shell in them are being attacked by algae. The Old Fort may crumble some day!

Therefore, just as you would check your home for physical termites, look for these termites in your husband-wife relationship: termites of unthoughtfulness, preoccupation, in-laws, unscriptural finances, poor appearance, television, addictive habits, adultery, and spiritual negligence.

The Cure for Divorce

Even when there have been repeated marital problems and threats of divorce, one is still shocked when a spouse asks for a divorce. Only the death of a spouse is more stressful than a breakup of a marriage. As a matter of fact, many of the symptoms accompanying death also are to be found surrounding divorce. My mother calls divorce a "living death." Some could have faced death easier than their mate with another person.

Passage Study

Before offering some practical suggestions to those threatened by divorce, look with me at a great passage of Scripture. We will not do an exhaustive exposition but will lift out some important principles.

In 1 Corinthians 7, there is a classic discussion of marriage. There are basically four sections: (1) precept of marriage (vv. 1-7), (2) permanence of marriage (vv. 8-16), (3) place of marriage (vv. 17-24), and (4) priorities of marriage (vv. 25-40). For our study, we will look at verses 1-17 and note the following principles:

- One of the purposes of marriage is to meet the sexual need (v. 2).
- It is wrong to sexually reject one's partner (vv. 3-5).
- Sexual needs should be met by each partner for his or her mate.

The only exception for these would involve possibly a crisis time where one or both mates needed to seek God. This is a "spiritual, sexual separation" with the following guidelines: (1) specific purpose—for prayer; (2) specific time—this should be agreed upon at the first so Satan would not be able to tempt them as their needs were not being met; and (3) specific spiritual conduct—fasting. These guidelines are found in verse 5.

I want to confess to you that I erroneously used this verse for years as a guideline for actual marital separation. For instance, a mate would come for counseling and want my blessing for a divorce. I would say, "I can never give a blessing for a divorce, but, maybe you need to be apart for a while." Then, I would show them the following guidelines in verse 5. How wrong I was! I now do not believe in separation, much less divorce! This verse only applies to married couples when a special time for prayer and seeking God's will are needed. God never wants the couple to be apart.

- There are some people with the gift of singleness (vv. 7-9). Paul was one whose calling from God was to be single. We should support our singles who do not feel it is God's will for them to be married. However, Paul says to singles: "If they cannot contain, let them marry: for it is better to marry than to burn" (v. 9).
- Notice God says two specific times: Do not divorce your mate, "put away" (vv. 11-12).
- Notice God says two specific times: Do not leave your mate (vv. 10,13).
- There are only two options for one whose marriage relationship is severed: remain single or be reconciled to the mate (v. 11). Remarriage is allowed in the Bible only in the case of the death of one's mate (Rom. 7:2-3).
- Although God's will was not followed in marrying an unbeliever (2 Cor. 6:14), the saved partner can be instrumental in bringing the unsaved spouse to Christ (2 Cor.7:13-14). God can use the saved spouse to spiritually affect the husband and children. There is hope for the unsaved because of the sanctifying possibilities of the saved spouse.
- There may come a time when the mate leaves. It is hard but "let him depart" (v. 15). Some have interpreted a part of this verse as acceptance of divorce: "A brother or a sister is not *under bondage* in such cases" (author's italics). This refers to our relationship to man, not God—divorce may happen, but we are still under God's law, not man's.
- If there is a separation, let it be peaceful (v. 15). Again, I confess my wrong counseling: I used to urge people to "fight for your marriage to the Supreme Court!" There are ways to "fight," but God "hath called us to peace" (v. 15). "The wrath of man worketh

not the righteousness of God" (Jas. 1:20). We'll fight God's way with God's weapons. Worked up hatred and bitterness can close the door to reconciliation.

Practical Suggestions

The following is what I would do if my mate asked me for a divorce.

Seek God.—When Jehoshaphat's crisis came, he "set himself to seek the Lord" (2 Chron. 20:3). Start getting your heart right with God. Make the pleasing of God your top priority (Prov. 16:7). Go to a quiet place (Matt. 6:6).

Confess all sins.—As you pray and seek God, He will reveal sins, flaws, and blind spots. Confess these (1 John 1:9). I have seen God clean up a mate and restore the joy to his or her life to the extent that he or she was attractive to the spouse again.

Make reconciliation with spouse.—The advice of James is pertinent. "Confess your faults one to another, and pray one for another, that ye may be healed" (5:16). A young wife called me one day, crying and distraught. Her husband had left her, and she freely admitted the fault was hers. I told her to be honest with him, take the blame, and promise restitution. She took this counsel, and the marriage was healed. Whatever God reveals to you about your faults—admit, confess, and vow with God's help to overcome shortcomings in character or conduct. Crises make us better or bitter.

Specific prayer.—You should pray. You should ask godly people whom you trust to pray, too. At our church, we have had a wonderful blessing in praying Hosea 2:6-7 about the estranged spouse. The person's parents, pastor, employer—any in authority over the person—should be asked to pray. Pray the principles of Hosea 2:6-7. Pray that God will hedge up his way with thorns. Pray that any counsel he is receiving from the world will sour and come to nought. Pray that he will be dissatisfied with the life apart from the marriage to the extent that he will desire to go back. As a matter of fact, pray that he will be pricked every way he turns, until he turns back home! This prayer works!

Do not gossip.—Do not badmouth your mate to family or friends. Let God be your defense as you "give place to wrath"

(Rom. 12:19). Talk to God. "He that repeateth a matter separateth very friends" (Prov. 17:9).

Ask God to show love through you.—We need His unconditional love in times like these. Love that "bears all things, believes all things, hopes all things, and endures all things" (1 Cor. 13:7, RSV). This love strengthens our commitment to our vows and God's way: We are more dedicated, disciplined, and determined.

Stay busy in service.—Don't be idle. Help others. Ventilate your energy in Christian service (Matt. 6:33; Heb.10:25).

Let your spouse go in peace.—Fight with prayer, faith in God's Word, kindness, and love. If it comes to the court case, let your spouse go in peace (1 Cor. 7:15). Bitterness will only increase the distance and possibly cause a marriage on the rebound. Hope to the end. Expect a miracle. "The things which are impossible with men are possible with God" (Luke 18:27). If the relationship is severed, we must and will go on living. God's purpose for your life continues. He will give you a ministry. He will reward you for remaining faithful to His Word.

A man decided to sell his house. Calling his realtor, he listed his house, describing it in detail. Then he set about to find another house for himself. For days he read the newspaper ads, and, one day, he saw the house of his dreams. Excitedly, he called his agent and told her about the ad he saw. There was silence on the other end. His realtor said, "Mr. Smith, the house you want is your house which you are trying to sell!" He was living in the kind of house he had always wanted.

Remain with your mate! You cannot do any better! Let God live and love through you.

10

What Should I Do When . . . I Am Lonely?

What a great man of God was the prophet Elijah! This man entered the ministry like a whirlwind into Ahab's court and left the ministry in a chariot of fire! God revealed His secret of the three-year drought to Elijah and the prophet courageously proclaimed the message to Israel and King Ahab. To Elijah belongs the distinction of being fed by ravens and given drink at mysteriously hidden brooks. Elijah was the undisputed spiritual champion of his time as he faced and defeated the prophets of Baal on Mount Carmel (1 Kings 18).

Upon coming to the nineteenth chapter of 1 Kings, however, we wonder what has happened to the mighty prophet. Here we find Elijah in a most miserable condition. He is discouraged, defeated, and lonely. There are many great principles in this account of Elijah, but we want to focus on the problem of loneliness. Hear Elijah as he says: "It is enough; now, O Lord, take away my life; for I am not better than my fathers" (v. 4). Read between the lines as God's former heavy-weight champion cries: "I, even I only, am left" (v. 14). Have you ever felt that way?

The Case of Loneliness

- Billy Graham has concluded that the one problem plaguing more people than any other is loneliness.
- Dr. Paul Tournier, eminent Swiss psychiatrist, has stated that loneliness is the most devastating malady of the age.
- In a poll of psychiatric patients it was found that more than 80 percent admitted that loneliness was the principal reason they sought help.
- Studies found in the majority of more than 500,000 attempt-

ed suicides that loneliness triggered the extreme action.

- A study at Alcoholics Anonymous revealed that many were driven to drinking by loneliness until alcohol became their uncontrollable escape.
- There is a marked increase in death among bereaved persons, especially during the first six months after the loss of a loved one.
- Divorced white men under the age of sixty-five have a higher death rate than married men of the same age. These divorced men have four times the car accidents, five times the suicides, and seven times the homicides. Loneliness is definitely a factor.

A widow called her lawyer to change her will. She told her lawyer that she wanted to be cremated. "Next," she requested, "I want my ashes to be dropped over Sears and Roebuck."

Shocked, the lawyer exclaimed, "Why do you want your ashes scattered over Sears and Roebuck?"

"Then," the lonely mother explained, "My children will come to see me at least twice a week!"

If the above story were not so truthful, it would be funny. There are many lonely people in the world.

Causes of Loneliness

Why are people lonely? Our lonely society has several influencing factors.

Mobility

Did you know that 20 percent of society moves every year? What a mobile society America is today! I know a pastor in a military town who can "lose" fifty families in a week due to transfers. Companies are increasingly aggressive in moving employees around the country for the betterment of business. Many people work hundreds of miles from home and are with their families only on weekends, sometimes not even then.

Mobility produces a sense of loneliness. For people to be happy, there must be a sense of stability. Friendships and meaningful relationships take time. A sense of community is provided by a network of friends who share similar interests and concerns. Today, people are like ships passing in the night with loneliness being the traumatic result.

Specialization

What dramatic changes are taking place in the business world! People are being replaced by machines and technological advances. Technical jobs make it difficult to feel a part of the team at work. It is easy to misunderstand the technical language that must be spoken today.

Do you feel the team concept at the place of your employment? Is there a sense of camaraderie where you work: One for all and all for one? I had a young man in my church who went to an outstanding university on a football scholarship. He mentioned that the team was divided into its specialities. The offensive line had its own coach and worked pretty much to themselves all week. This was true with the offensive backfield, defensive line, defensive backfield, and specialty teams. All were so specialized that they did not feel part of the team until game time—then, there was the unbelievable pressure to succeed that took the fun out of the game! For many today, specialization at work has choked the fun out of the game and created a social loneliness that is devastating.

Impersonalization

Very closely akin to specialization is the cause of impersonalization. The business world seemingly considers only the "bottom line" of profit and production. We received members from another city where the woman worked as a nurse for a world-famous hospital. She told me that she was told the priorities of the hospital at the beginning of her employment. They were as follows: research, education, then people. The emphasis was on production not people—in a hospital!

I remember a college football coach who was famous for his "tower" during the practices. The coach would oversee the practices from his tower and remain an imposing figure even when his feet were on the ground. Management in many businesses today make people feel like means to an end. Loneliness is created when human beings do not see or feel their worth.

I believe the closest I've ever come to being lonely was on registration days at new schools. I stood in a line fifty yards long in front of the letters "A to I." Then I filled out page after page of biographical questions and was finally given a number which identified me the rest of my college days. My grades were posted with the number. My bills came via the number. I became a number!

Recently we hired a new part-time custodian at church. I was working late one night, and my daughter was with me. She came running to my office saying she had seen a man in the halls whom she did not know. I went looking for him and found him just as he was starting to get into his car and drive home for the night. I called to him, "Hey! Are you looking for somebody?"

This man turned back toward me and hollered, "I am somebody!" He was right. We all are somebody and impersonalization takes away our sense of worth.

Television

Did you know the average American household has the television on for almost seven hours a day? The television is America's number one baby-sitter. Due to the power of the television, families can sit for hours and never speak to one another. Television is hypnotic, leading one to waste much valuable time each day as one sits under its spell.

Because we let television do the talking, we never talk to one another. People have forgotten how to think for themselves and now permit the television to determine their thought patterns and behavior. Television takes us away from our own vital, real world into worlds of fantasy and make-believe. In another chapter on aging, we learn that senior adults feel that television is absolutely vital to their lives. If the television did not talk to them, they could not make it through the day. What a shame! A television can not take the place of people. Turn off the television!

Urbanization

We have almost lost the "country closeness" of yesterday! Urbanization has created neighborhoods of strangers. People are afraid of being mugged. Because of fear, people do not slow down long enough to make friends and form meaningful relationships. The needs for privacy and protection make us want to be alone.

Years ago, I read a study of the most vandalized subdivisions in America. Several characteristics were given, including poor lighting, secluded streets, and bulky bushes in the yards. But, the number one reason was that these subdivisions were neighborhoods of strangers. They did not know one another and did not feel responsible for one another. Tragedies can happen in our own subdivisions among families, and we do not know about them until it is too late to offer support.

There are basically three types of loneliness: (1) *Common Loneliness*—This is the cyclical type which comes with holiday seasons, job failure, transiency, and the change in emotions. (2) *Crisis Loneliness*—This takes place when there is a sudden change in our life. A death or loss can drive one into deep, prolonged loneliness. (3) *Chronic Loneliness*—This type arises from negative feelings of self-esteem or deep internal conflict. Usually, this person feels profoundly anxious or depressed on a regular basis.

Two widows were talking one day. One said, "Being alone does so color one's life, doesn't it?"

The other woman, a godly person, replied, "Yes, but isn't it nice that we can choose our colors!" Examine the list of causes for loneliness. Do any of these fit your life situation? Determine, with God's help, that you are going to start choosing your own colors.

Characteristics of Loneliness

There are several key characteristics of loneliness which should prove to be most revealing.

Loneliness Strikes Without Regard for Age

This dreaded malady is no respecter of persons. *Small children* exhibit loneliness today: Working parents have little time for their children. We're producing a latch-key generation. Baby-sitters, day-care, and preschools are full. Studies indicate the most prevalent cause of crying during the first three months is loneliness. *Teenagers* feel misunderstood and alienated from their elders. Youth feel most lonely on Friday and Saturday nights. This feeling of loneliness can bring hasty relationships and premature marriages. *College students* feel lonely in a place where they do not know people well yet. The first time away from home can be heartbreaking. *Service people,* sometimes thrown in with an ungodly bunch, are lonely. *Married* folks, even in the most intimate of relationships, exhibit devastating characteristics of loneliness. The most difficult alcoholic to smoke out is one in a lonely house. The *aged* feel useless and unwanted. Loneliness has no age restrictions.

Loneliness Strikes at Many Different Times

We expect loneliness upon coming home to an empty house after the death of a spouse or parent. Loneliness also can be shocking when the last child leaves home. Loneliness can attack on sunny days as well as dark days.

Loneliness Is a Condition of the Heart, Not Numbers

Immersing ourselves in a crowd is no cure for loneliness. In one year the average American today probably meets as many people as the average person did in a lifetime 100 years ago. No other people run so hard to keep from being alone than Americans. But, the sad truth is, you can be lonely among a crowd of people. I heard a former president of the Southern Baptist Convention say that the loneliest he has ever felt was walking down the halls of the Southern Baptist Convention! Seeing all those people—and, yet, not enjoying a personal relationship with most of them. Being in a crowd does not solve our loneliness problem.

Loneliness Is Different than Aloneness

Aloneness and loneliness are far from being the same. Aloneness may bring on loneliness, but it need not. We need times of aloneness, don't we? When was the last time you were a chaperone on a youth retreat? I tell you, you can have youth all over you just so long! Then, you're willing even to skip a meal—just to have the luxury of sitting under a tree with some peace and quiet! I heard about a housewife who had ten children. The only time she could be alone was when she stood in the middle of the kitchen floor and pulled her apron up over her head!

We need times of aloneness: "He leadeth me beside the still waters. He restoreth my soul" (Ps. 23:2-3). David used his times of aloneness to prepare for his coming battles of life. I believe

Daniel's prayer times with the Lord enabled him to interpret dreams and courageously face the lions. Moses spent forty years on the back side of the desert becoming God's man for the exodus. The secret of power comes from the private place not the public place. We need aloneness.

Our Lord Jesus showed us the example concerning aloneness. See Him alone for forty days battling the devil (Matt. 4). Notice how many times Jesus went to the desert or to the top of a mountain to pray. Hear Jesus evaluate His life-style: "Foxes have holes, and the birds of the air have nests; but the Son of man hath not where to lay his head" (Matt. 8:20). See our Lord as He prays and sweats in the garden of Gethsemane (Matt. 26:36-46). And, in the epitome of aloneness, hear Jesus cry: "My God, my God, why hast thou forsaken me?" (Matt. 27:46)

Yes, there is a difference between aloneness and loneliness. You need to be alone for Bible study, prayer, and communion with God. Remember where Jesus said for us to pray? "Enter into thy *closet,* and when thou hast shut thy door, pray to thy Father which is in *secret;* and thy Father which seeth in *secret* shall reward thee openly" (Matt. 6:6, author's italics). Yes, we need to go into our closet and be alone with our Heavenly Father. Use the times of aloneness creatively, and you will have fewer times of loneliness.

Cure for Loneliness

Remember leaving Elijah beneath a juniper tree, alone, and requesting God to take his life. The prophet had run into the response to Queen Jezebel's threat upon his life (1 Kings 19:2). Now, he is alone and lonely. The Scripture gives some beautiful descriptions of the way God cared for Elijah:

- God put him to sleep (vv. 5-8). Sleep is a marvelous cure. It is amazing how differently troubles look after a good night's sleep. God graciously put the prophet to sleep. Fatigue makes cowards of us all.
- God woke him, fed him, and put him to sleep again (v. 6). Mysteriously, God prepared him a hot meal. Then, He knocked Elijah out again for some more rest.
- Again, God woke him and fed him (vv. 7-8).

• After leading Elijah on a journey to a specific place, God asked the prophet a piercing question: "What doest thou here, Elijah?" (v. 9) God wanted Elijah to analyze his condition. The Lord is about to teach the prophet a valuable lesson. The following are three specific cures for loneliness.

God's Presence in Your Life

You can read verses 9-12 and see the experience Elijah had with God. The first cure God wanted to emphasize was His presence with the prophet. "Elijah, you're not alone! You're not in this by yourself. I am with you." I had a member once who had an awful experience in World War II. The fighting was horrible beyond words. As loneliness was about to set in to chill my member's bones, he said the forty-sixth Psalm came to him. Put yourself in his position and read that remarkable Psalm. It begins with the words, "God is our refuge and strength, a very present help in trouble" (v. 1). Awful calamities are described that happened to the psalmist. Then, the words: "Be still, and know that I am God" (v. 10). The church member could still quote that psalm after forty years. How he testified of how God's presence comforted him in his loneliness.

When Satan tempts you into thinking you are abandoned, realize God is with you. Whether you are on the hospital bed, in a jail cell, on a witness stand, beside a grave, or in an empty house, God is with you! He will never leave or forsake you. Do you remember how worried Moses was about leading the people of God? Time after time God had to assure His servant: "My presence shall go with thee, and I will give thee rest" (Ex. 33:14). The first part of our cure for loneliness is to realize we are never alone: God is always with us.

God's Purpose for Your Life

Elijah was told to get back into society where people's needs were. The prophet was told in verse 15 to go and anoint Hazael to be king over Syria. He was told to anoint Jehu to be king over Israel. Further, Elijah was commanded to anoint Elisha to be a future leader of the prophets (v. 16). Wow! God wasn't finished with Elijah yet, was He! Anointing two kings and a future spiritual leader was a great commission.

God has a wonderful purpose for your life. You do not have time to be lonely! Get your mind off yourself—there are emptier cups than yours. Multiply yourself. Make sure the work of God will go on when you are gone. Produce living monuments. "Be ye doers of the word" (Jas. 1:22).

I pastored the most amazing woman in South Louisiana. She was affectionately called "Aunt Bertie," and she certainly was everyone's aunt! The mother of six children, and having faced the destructive South Louisiana hurricanes for seventy years, it did not daunted her when I became her pastor. Aunt Bertie sang in the choir (provided special music, too), taught a women's Sunday School class, and was the director of Vacation Bible School each year. She also sent a birthday card to every child in the Louisiana Baptist Children's Home for many years. I honestly believe that, if you had taken any of the positions of service away from Aunt Bertie, you would have killed her! She lived to serve and served to live.

Knowing God has a purpose for our lives should keep loneliness away. "Every branch in me that beareth not fruit he taketh away" (John 15:2). Invest your life in the lives of others. Start today!

God's People in Your Life

Do you remember that Elijah whined, "And I, even I only, am left" (v. 14). Well, God deals with that excuse for loneliness in verse 18: "Yet I have left me seven thousand in Israel, all the knees which have not bowed unto Baal, and every mouth which hath not kissed him." The prophet was told by God that He still had people with whom he could fellowship—no cause for Elijah to be lonely.

Thank God for the fellowship of the church. The church is never a place but always a people; never a fold but always a flock; never a sacred building but always a believing assembly. God saw the first man and said: "It is not good that the man should be alone" (Gen. 2:18). Just as Adam was given one with whom he could fellowship, so the child of God finds love and fellowship within the spiritual bride of Christ, the church.

Are you faithful in the services of God's church? (Heb. 10:25). You need the fellowship of the people of God: "Iron sharpeneth iron; so a man sharpeneth the countenance of his friend" (Prov. 27:17). You no doubt have discovered that your relatives in Christ can be closer oftentimes than your physical family. "Whosoever shall do the will of my Father which is in heaven, the same is my brother, and sister, and mother" (Matt. 12:50). Do maintain your right and privilege with the people of God.

What should I do when I am lonely? I believe the most inspirational model I've ever seen in dealing with loneliness is my own mother. My parents divorced when I was eighteen years old. My mother has often said that divorce is like living death. She never remarried but has lived for God and her children. The world is not kind or merciful toward the unprotected widow or divorcee, but my mother has been great. She has modeled the cures that I have shared with you:

- The Lord's *presence* in her life has gotten stronger and more real over the years. She is very close to Jesus! She has blessed my people when I ask her to pray for our church.
- The Lord's *purpose* for her life has increased and become more vivid over the years. I do not ever remember her as active in God's service as she is now at seventy years of age. She plays the church piano, teaches a Sunday School class for little children, and works in the bus ministry. She does not have time to get lonely!
- The Lord's *people* around her life have been an untold blessing. Mother has attended a Bible class during the week for several years, which has been good for her. She has special Christian women friends with whom she prays, studies, worships, and fellowships. They are such a happy, holy group!

Don't give in to loneliness! Claim God's presence. Find God's purpose for your life. Join and enjoy God's people.

11

What Should I Do When . . . I Am Tempted to Commit Adultery?

Adultery has been called the "scarlet sin." Adultery has broken up more homes than any other sin. Adultery stabs the heart of God, shocks the church, and severs the peace of congregations. A national magazine's headlines read: "Infidelity on the Rampage." Has there ever been a generation when marriage vows were so disregarded and divorce so easy?"

The young couple sat nervously in front of a pastor whom they had never met before that evening. They needed someone who would be objective, yet spiritual, to hear their story and tell them God's solution. The woman spoke first. Her words gushed with bitterness and authority as she told of her mate's adulterous affair. Her husband, a manager of a food store, had become attracted to one of his employees. Infatuation had led to adultery as the couple had gone to North Carolina for a weekend together. The wife related how this had happened before in their marriage, and she had been willing to forgive and forget. The husband hung his head as the wife stated her demands, if the marriage were to be saved. Her demands were to fire the woman or get another job, get an AIDS test, and go to church with her and the children.

The husband, when allowed to speak, admitted everything. He wanted more than anything to save his marriage. He said, "Pastor, it's like I've got a sickness. I love my wife and family. What should I do when I'm tempted by another person?"

What great man said this: "Women are married to be divorced, and divorced to be married?" What man of wisdom said: "We keep prostitutes for pleasure; we keep mistresses for the day to day needs of the body; we keep wives for the begetting of children and for the faithful guardianship of our homes?" The first statement was by Seneca and the second by Demosthenes. These men spoke of the moral situations in their day which was over 2,000 years ago. They might as well have been talking about our generation! We have storms on today's homes.

In dealing with this needful subject, this chapter is organized into these parts: characteristics, causes, a case study, and (4) the cure.

Characteristics of Adultery

Read carefully the following facts, quotes, and observations.

- Adultery is defined as unlawful sexual relations with the spouse of another. Adultery is found mentioned over seventy times in the Bible. Fornication is found forty-four times in the Scriptures.
- Sex scandals have rocked Capitol Hill in Washington, D.C. A professor was quoted in the newspaper: "A safe bet would be that nearly half the members of Congress have been involved in affairs outside of marriage."
- Estimates range from 33 percent to 50 percent of marriages ending in divorce.
- There is an increasing incidence of extramarital affairs among professing Christians.
- Estimates say that 72 percent of married men have had affairs.
- More than 50 percent of single professional women had an affair in 1985 with a coworker or client. (In 1984, it was 17 percent.)
- Women who engaged in premarital sex would be more apt than other women in having affairs.
- Wage-earning wives had noticeable higher incidence of marital unfaithfulness than homemakers.
- Nonreligious wives are twice as likely as religious wives to have sex with other men.
- How twisted our society has become! What was once labeled adultery is now an *affair*—a nice-sounding, almost inviting word wrapped in mystery, fascination, and excitement. An affair has become a relationship, not sin. What was once behind the scenes,

a closely guarded secret, is now in the headlines, a TV theme, a best-seller, and as common as the cold.

- To marriage, this says faithfulness is out; affairs are in. If your marriage doesn't provide at all times all you've ever expected, dreamed, or fantasized and if it fails to bring you the constant sensual pleasure and fulfillment you deserve, find it elsewhere! Enjoy some healthy adultery! No regulations and no relationships!
- Our culture is at the point of total saturation about sex. The cesspool is running over. Books, magazines, billboards, TV, and movies shout it endlessly. Sex gets the ratings. It is the recurring theme in the daytime soaps and talk shows. Sex is the inevitable subject in the nighttime interviews.
- "Healthy" adultery is now urged by counselors, psychologists, and sexologists. Couples, whose romantic love has faded, are urged to try adultery to rejuvenate their relationships.
- Worldly counselors have no suggestions on how to build love again, just a self-centered answer. Go outside—have an affair!
- A brilliant lawyer from a major Tennessee city told me that the number one reason for marriages breaking up was adultery. He said his firm overwhelmingly agreed that the unfaithfulness of a marriage partner (usually the man) had been used as the reason to file for divorce more than any other.

Causes of Adultery

Why would people break God's commandment, ruin their name, endanger their home, and risk contracting sexual diseases?

Emotional Immaturity

In many cases, the sin has been committed by a partner who has never grown up. Obedience to God or parents was never learned. They are not faithful or disciplined in any of their relationships. Probably this person was never told "no" by permissive parents. The culprit in adultery is an adult who still has the roving eye and the flirty personality: "I'm just not a one-woman man!"

A person who does the following has not acquired adult or

Christian values:

- Goes to places of temptation.
- Reads *Playboy* or other worldly magazines and adult books.
- Attends R- or X-rated movies.
- Listens to and tells dirty jokes.

Unresolved Conflict

All marriages will have conflict and stress. Where adultery has invaded a home, many times there have been conflicts which have gone unsolved. As these become larger, their love is not strong enough to cover the weaknesses. Of course, during this time healthy communication is almost nonexistent. To relieve tension, an affair takes place.

Many times the conflict can center around the job. With the husband, work is everything. The wife feels rejection and expresses herself about love and romance: A language most husbands do not understand!

Unmet Needs

In my ministry, I have had few husbands who have come and said to me: "My wife just does not love me. What can I do to win her back?" First of all, usually the wife is the one initiating help for the relationship. Secondly, a wife usually takes abuse and neglect over a period of years before she makes her "break." All of this time the man is totally oblivious that any problem exists. He thinks any problem can be remedied by sex or an "I'm sorry." In most relationships, both partners take one another for granted. Because the man has so many outside interests, he is able to ventilate his frustrations and find outlets to work this out. The wife, however, finds most of her self-esteem centering around her husband and the home. When her marriage relationship is not healthy, this becomes a problem of grave concern to the entire family.

Affection is needed in a marriage. I heard about an unhappy couple who was robbed one day. The thief frisked both of them and was amazed at how little money they had. The woman said, "If you will frisk me again, I'll write you a check!" A little display of affection goes a long way. Most of us want and are starved for affection. The problem here, however, is that most men interpret affection as a "come on" and start thinking "sex." The men have not learned to love without emphasizing sex.

Verbal praise would go far in meeting needs. A precious relationship can be torn down by excessive nagging and criticism (Prov. 21:19; 26:21; 27:15). I heard Art Linkletter say that, for every one negative comment to a child, four positive comments are needed to keep a balance. Again, most men do not know how to say, "I love you." And, because their love and praise are not reciprocated, women eventually tire of doing it themselves. Let's us learn to compliment, praise, and encourage our mate! Attention nourishes a relationship.

How Does an Affair Happen?

Let me give several criteria of how an affair takes place.

(1) Spiritual weakness from within at first.

(2) Unhappiness in the home, needs not being met, unresolved conflict, and communication not adequately taking place.

(3) Temptation with outside person takes place. Could be at work, at business, in the neighborhood, or at church! It starts innocently:

- Someone shows attention and interest and admiration.
- This feels good since the needs are not being met at home. We need admiration and affection from someone!
- Soon activities are provided with that person.
- Our minds create a fantasy—a mental picture captivates our minds about going to bed with that person.
- Our fantasy creates the emotions, and the emotions scream for the actual experience. This is why when one is emotionally committed to an affair, all the truth and logic doesn't seem to faze him.

(4) The marriage partner becomes passive. The fantasy cannot be fed on the home front.

(5) Comparison breeds contempt. There is no way a wife in an apron can compare to the beautiful woman at work being paid to dress and act nice! All areas of home life are criticized—food, sex, clothing, and total atmosphere.

(6) The consequences are considered. The "grass is greener" on

the other side. The man leaves the home in separation. Divorce is filed for and usually attained amid much bitterness.

Causes of Adultery

Example of Joseph

The most vivid portrait of an adulterous temptation in the Bible can be found in Genesis 39. You will remember that Joseph has been sold into slavery by his brothers. He finds himself in the home of a man named Potiphar. Potiphar had position and prosperity as he was an officer of Pharaoh. He also had a wife who figured prominently in the life and future of Joseph.

We read that God blessed Potiphar through Joseph's employment (v. 5). God had anointed Joseph in the area of business management, and Potiphar made him "overseer of his house, and all that he had he put into his hand" (v. 4). Joseph's business ability and personality, coupled with his good looks (v. 6), made him an attractive young man. How clearly the Bible presents the temptation made to Joseph by Potiphar's wife! Probably after flirtatious glances and tantalizing remarks, Potiphar's wife bluntly offered herself to Joseph: "Lie with me" (v. 7). Joseph refused, saying this sin would be disobedience to God and dishonoring to Potiphar, who trusted him (vv. 8-9). The wife of Potiphar tried again, however, at an opportune time when the house was empty. Again, Joseph refused and incurred the fury of a scorned woman, resulting in imprisonment.

It is interesting to note several reasons why this sin could have been attractive to Joseph. The following is how Joseph might have rationalized.

Everyone does it.—The Egyptians were famous for their lack of morals. The philosophy of the world at that time, as Demosthenes said, was to have prostitutes for pleasure, mistresses for day-to-day needs, and wives for beginning and maintaining a family. In Joseph's day, there was nothing wrong with an affair by a man as long as he supported his wife and family. In short, everyone was doing it. Joseph could have rationalized: "I am no different than anyone else. I am away from my home land and in a land where extramarital sex is sanctioned. Why should I deny myself and forfeit this opportunity of pleasure?"

Today's society operates on the same principle. Everywhere we turn, sex is sensationalized. Ninety-five percent of the sexual situations on television are immoral. Sex and sensuality sell everything from clothes to perfume. Convictions are shattered in people's minds and hearts as we see a whole society doing their thing. The sad fact that visible Christian preachers have had affairs further weakens people's convictions. Joseph could have committed this sin with Potiphar's wife, and society would not have condemned him for it.

No one would know.—Potiphar's wife secured the perfect opportunity: No one was in the house (v. 11). Her husband was gone; the men were gone—no one would ever know! She and Joseph could slip into bed, and no one on earth would ever find out—a perfect situation.

How many have been lured into sin thinking no one would ever know? King David committed sin with a beautiful woman, Bathsheba, and thought no one would ever know. However, she became pregnant with his child while her husband was away fighting for Israel and David. To cover his sin, David resorted to the murder of Bathsheba's faithful husband, Uriah. Each year thousands of teenage girls became pregnant. They thought a moment's pleasure would never be revealed. A pregnancy is not an easy sin to hide!

Joseph knew that "the eyes of the Lord are in every place, beholding the evil and the good" (Prov. 15:3). He knew all sin was against God, and he could hear God say: "Be sure your sin will find you out" (Num. 32:23). People plan the perfect sin, as a husband doing wrong while on a business trip, but they forget about God! "Be not deceived; God is not mocked: for whatsoever a man soweth, that shall he also reap" (Gal. 6:7).

The woman's personal invitation.—Sin usually has a sequence. In this case, probably there were flirtatious looks and tantalizing remarks. Potiphar's wife may have worn special clothing to tempt Joseph. A touch or some form of closeness will break down barriers. But, notice that the woman gave Joseph a personal invitation (vv. 7,12). Discretion and honor are abandoned as the wife of Potiphar threw herself at Joseph.

When a woman is aggressive, men are practically powerless in their resistance. Any man would surely be tried if a beautiful woman offered herself to him day after day. Today's society has reached a place where I am especially alarmed about the loss of shame and respect in womanhood. I realize a man is as accountable for society's standards as the woman (if not more!). However, when the women become "easy" and even aggressive in sexual behavior toward men, there will be affairs, pregnancies, and trouble! Single men in my church speak often as to the growing availability of women today for sexual pleasure. This temptation was most attractive because of the woman's personal invitation.

Ministry to the woman.—There is a fourth reason why sexual immorality might have been attractive to Joseph. This reason will not be seen by the average Bible student in the Genesis 39 account. Notice that Potiphar is called an "officer of Pharaoh" in verse 1. This word, *officer*, can have reference to the position of a eunuch. History records that rulers often made eunuchs out of those who were in intimate positions at the royal court. This is sheer speculation, but it could have been, then, that Potiphar was physically unable to meet the needs of his wife. Sex may have been an unsatisfactory part of their marriage.

Joseph could have rationalized: "Poor Mrs. Potiphar, going through life unable to know the satisfaction of sexual fulfillment—what would be wrong if I 'ministered' to her and helped her have some enjoyment in life?" Hey! Don't laugh! Have you ever talked to someone who had an affair at the office? Chances are, this affair began as a "ministry" where they began to listen to the sob stories of the other. Both bad-mouthed their mates and cried on one another's shoulder. Both sympathized with the other and how neither of them were being fulfilled in life. Soon, a pat becomes a pet! This happens all the time between employers and employees. This offers firm evidence that a secretary or boss should never be allowed to meet needs that one's mate would meet. Much adultery comes in the way of sympathy or as a ministry. This reason could have made the sin of immorality most attractive to Joseph.

Exhortation of 1 Thessalonians 4:3-8

With the vivid example of Joseph in mind, let us apply the exhortation of Paul in 1 Thessalonians 4:3-8. Paul gives seven reasons why the Christian should not commit sexual immorality.

Not following God's will.—God's will is and always has been holiness and purity. Notice verse 3: "For this is the *will of God*, even your sanctification, that ye should *abstain* from fornication" (author's italics). Sexual sin is not God's will. The Seventh Commandment is: "Thou shalt not commit adultery" (Ex. 20:14). We should want to please God by doing His will!

Dishonors the body.—*Posses* in verse 4 means to control. We should live a holy life-style and learn the habit of purity. Our body should be controlled and devoted to honor and not dishonor. Immorality dishonors the body, because unbridled passion and lust is controlling the body when this sin is committed. We must not be dominated by sin.

Provides wrong marriage motive.—The word *vessel*, in verse 4 may mean our body, but it also could mean the person's mate. Therefore, "possess his vessel in sanctification and honor" may refer to conducting marriage and courtship in a holy way that honors God. The Gentiles were dominated by lust and passion (v. 5), and Paul wrote that marriage should have an honorable motive. Commitment to God and one another should come before passion and emotions of lust. If sex is indulged before marriage, the body is placed before the Spirit. A dark cloud of guilt covers that relationship until confessed and forgiven.

Is sin against others.—Verse 6 mentions how sexual immorality "defrauds" one's brother. *Defraud* means to rob, cheat, or take advantage. Sexual immorality takes what belongs to another. Joseph would not sin with Potiphar's wife, because she belonged to another (Gen. 39:9). I find it amusing that boys feel they must sow their wild oats, and, yet, when they start looking for a wife, they want a virgin. God's original plan called for one man for one woman for life. We sin against our brother when sexual immorality is committed.

Leads to punishment from God.—The Scripture says in verse 6 that "the Lord is the avenger of all such." In the Old Testament, adultery was punished by death. Sin has its built-in punishment and sexual immorality is no different! One of my favorite cartoons showed Beetle Bailey talking to his chaplain: "First it was V.D., then Herpes. Now it's AIDS. What does it all mean, Chaplain?"

The Chaplain wisely replies, "It means God doesn't fool around and neither should you!" God was the Avenger when David committed adultery. God will punish when people indulge in the sin of adultery. See Proverbs 6:30-35.

Does not follow the call of God.—What is the call of God? He has called us to holiness, not uncleanness (v. 7). After conversion, we realize we're different: A new nature has been implanted. Through that new nature, we are "called" to holiness. We cannot sin any more and enjoy it. Our new nature urges us to want to live a holy life and, through God's power, we can live a holy life. Paul is saying, "What are you doing? You know the call of God. You know you are doing wrong! Abstain from fornication. That is not what God has called you to do!" Committing this sin goes against the purpose of conversion.

Rebels against God.—If we persist in committing the sin of immorality, it comes down to outright rebellion. Verse 8 says that the man who sins "despiseth not man, but God, who hath also given unto us his Holy Spirit." *Despiseth* can also mean rejects. The adulterer treats the commands of God as though they are as nothing. It is to declare to God: "I do not care about You. I will not be bound by your Commandments." The sin of adultery shows contempt for divine authority.

Each of Paul's reasons for staying pure can be found in the example of Joseph. Feeling the *call of God* in his life, he knew it was not *God's will* to *dishonor his body*. Joseph would be *sinning against another* if he committed adultery, and he wanted to *save himself for marriage*. God would *punish* if he *rebelled*.

The Cure for Adultery

Many of the cures for the temptation to commit adultery have been mentioned already in the chapter. Stating the causes positively can be a starting point for the cures. Notice some of these principles:

• Expect and prepare for temptation. Realize that you will be tempted. The right person with all the right ingredients will come across your path one day. You must develop a biblical conscience.

• Build up your spiritual heart. "Be strong in the Lord, and in the power of his might" (Eph. 6:10). "Put on the whole armor of God, that ye may be able to stand against the wiles of the devil" (v. 11). David was not strong spiritually, when the incident with Bathsheba happened in his life.

• Give yourself to your marriage. Remember that "love" is spelled T-I-M-E. Work at developing your relationship with your wife. Put your priorities in order: Next to God, your mate should come first in life.

• Examine your relationship in these areas. Look at how you are as a mate in your attention, affections, admiration, and activities.

• Do not flirt. "He winketh with his eyes, he speaketh with his feet, he teacheth with his fingers" (Prov. 6:13). These are characteristics of a naughty person, a wicked man.

• Watch your clothing. Clothing is to cover our nakedness not serve as a lure and trap for the opposite sex. Men should watch their tight trousers. Women should guard against the low blouses and high skirts. "Abstain from all appearance of evil" (1 Thess. 5:22).

• If attracted to someone, remove yourself immediately. Don't allow yourself to be alone with them again. Joseph fled and left his coat in Potiphar's wife's hand (Gen. 39:12). The Bible says: "Flee also youthful lusts" (2 Tim. 2:22). You may have to request a transfer or leave your job. You may have to talk firmly and spiritually to the person—break the relationship now!

• Be careful about friendships. Usually there is an element of romance in affairs. Do not share any of your intimate problems with the opposite sex. Intimacy of soul takes place when one shares intimate feelings. Talk to your own mate!

• There is always a way of escape. You will not face a temptation which you can't overcome: "There hath no temptation taken you but such as is common to man: but God is faithful, who will not suffer you to be tempted above that ye are able; but will with the temptation also make a *way* to *escape*, that ye may be able to bear it" (1 Cor. 10:13, author's italics). Do pray and ask Him for strength. I have heard so many say, "If I had known then what I know now, I could have saved my marriage." Stay in there! God will provide a way for you to do His will. Romans 8:28 is still true.

• Consider the consequences. How sin blinds the sinner! Haven't you seen people indulged in adultery simply act like children! They do not realize people know—sin deceives people. Adulterers do not consider their family—the relationship to their faithful mates and their children. Always the children are the most to suffer when an adulterous relationship happens. Adultery does not consider the cost to one's name. Also, the reproach upon the name of Christ is never considered. Sin is so selfish, so self-gratifying, that people have thrown away their whole families and fortunes. Look down the road far enough to see how your sin would impact your family, name, future, and the cause of Christ.

• Do not feed the flesh. Avoid books, movies, television programs, and other matters of sexual content. These defile the imagination and inflame the passions. People caught in adultery have admitted how Satan used various indulgences to keep the passions inflamed. Burn all bad books or movies!

• Control your thoughts. "As he thinketh in his heart, so is he" (Prov. 23:7). Garbage in, garbage out. Resist fantasizing and comparing your mate with other persons. We must bring "into captivity every thought to the obedience of Christ" (2 Cor. 10:5).

Jesus called His generation an "adulterous and sinful generation" (Mark 8:38). God helps us in the midst of our adulterous and sinful generation to be a "royal priesthood, an holy nation, and a peculiar people" (1 Pet. 2:9).

12

What Should I Do When . . . I Don't Know God's Will?

The man entered the pastor's office with a distraught look on his face. The ensuing conversation revealed that he had been offered another position with his company. But accepting this position would involve moving to another region of the country. "Pastor," the man explained, "This is what I've prayed for! This job has a dramatic increase in salary and benefits. I will be in line after this position for a top management place in the company." However, examining the other side showed that he and his wife would be leaving both their parents, the school which their children enjoyed, and the church which had shown them the way to salvation and service. The confused husband and father said to his pastor: "What should I do when I don't know God's will?"

A sweet Christian girl has fallen in love with a young man who had asked her to marry him. She is concerned that he is not a Christian. Should she marry him and trust God to work through her to win him to faith in Christ? Or, should she break off the relationship? Or, should she put God on a timetable and see how the relationship looks in six months?

A young man is graduating from high school and wants to go to college. Should he go to a state school or a Christian college?

A concerned couple confided in their prayer group that they did not know if they should have any more children. The wife is in her mid-thirties and feels that they need to make a decision soon because of her age. However, she has had health problems which accompanied the birth of her last child. The painful question surfaced again: "What should we do when we don't know God's will?"

Surely one of the predominant pastoral problems is helping God's people find His will for their lives. Hardly a week does not go by without some member posing some form of this question to a pastor: "What should I do when I don't know God's will?" Pastors had better know how to enable their flock to follow the Good Shepherd!

George W. Truett pointed out: "To know the will of God is the greatest knowledge. To do the will of God is the greatest experience."

F. B. Meyer stated: "Peace consists in knowing where God would have us be, and in being just there."

The desire of every child of God should be to find God's will and remain in God's will. Peter said the Christian "should no longer live the rest of his time in the flesh to the lusts of men, but to the will of God" (1 Pet. 4:2). The happiest place, the safest place, is God's will. "He that doeth the will of God abideth for ever" (1 John 2:17).

This chapter is dedicated to helping find God's perfect will for our lives. We will examine: cases of God's will, consequences of being out of His will, and the cure.

Cases of God's Will

Wouldn't it be wonderful if finding God's will were like the example we have of the children of Israel? When the Israelites broke free of the Egyptians, "the Lord went before them by day in a pillar of a cloud, to lead them the way; and by night in a pillar of fire, to give them light; to go by day and night" (Ex. 13:21). How marvelous! There was never any doubt as to where God was or what He was doing. Watch the cloud! We remember that, when the cloud rested on the tabernacle, the nation stayed at rest and did not move. However, when the cloud was taken from the tabernacle, then they journeyed and followed the cloud (Num. 9:15-23). Of course, the cloud represented God's presence and was used to guide an entire nation through an uncharted territory. We want our obedience to be this way, also. When God moves, we move. When God stays, we stay. Whatever God is doing, we want to be with Him.

Another wonderful case of God's will involves the prophet

Elijah. Remember that Elijah burst into the court of King Ahab, announced a coming drought, and then went into hiding for three and one-half years. He was a marked man. He was on the move constantly because of Ahab's soldiers and the effects of the drought. Read the seventeenth chapter of 1 Kings and count the number of times *there* is mentioned. Upon leaving Ahab's court, God told him to go eastward and hide at the brook Cherith: "I have commanded the ravens to feed thee *there*" (v. 4, author's italics). God gave his prophet water while the rest of the country perished. He fed him by way of scavenger birds which would not attract attention during those death-filled times. After a while, God moved Elijah to Zarephath: "Behold, I have commanded a widow woman *there* to sustain thee" (v. 9, author's italics). Again, God protected and provided for His servant through showing him His will. The "there" of God's will is the safest and happiest place on earth for us. Are you "there" right now in God's will?

Have you ever heard how John Wesley found a wife? He first fell in love with a girl named Sophia. Not knowing if marriage to her was God's will, he called his Holy Club together, drew lots, and Sophia was history! Next, he fell in love with a widow and Bible teacher named Grace Murray. This time he used a common-sense method by listing her pros and cons. Feeling she was God's will, he was about to enter into marriage when his brother, Charles, intervened. Charles visited Grace and fainted at her feet, causing her to change her mind about John. Finally, a year and a half later, at the age of forty-seven, John did marry a wealthy widow named Mary Vazeille. While we do not know the method he used to determine God's will, their marriage was very unhappy. She left him after twenty years of marriage. Even a man of John Wesley's spiritual stature could err about the will of God.

Jesus should be our example in following God's will. What a wonderful life our Lord had on earth. His consuming desire was to do the will of His Father in heaven, as is shown in the following verses:

- "My meat is to do the will of him that sent me, and to finish his work" (John 4:34).
- "I seek not mine own will, but the will of the Father which hath sent me" (John 5:30).

• "For I came down from heaven, not to do mine own will, but the will of him that sent me" (John 6:38).

• As the time neared for the suffering to begin, our Lord prayed to His Father in the garden of Gethsemane: "Father, if thou be willing, remove this cup from me: nevertheless not my will, but thine, be done" (Luke 22:42).

Our Lord, because He was following His Father's will, always was in the right place at the right time. Seemingly, He never altered His schedule: He prayed, set His course, and God brought the people across His path. He was at the well when a needy woman came (John 4). He was at the pool of Bethesda to reach a crippled man (John 5). Jesus lived on a divine timetable which was the will of God. He kept the feasts, performed His ministry, went to the cross, died, was buried, arose, remained on earth for forty days, and ascended. Truly, our Lord shows us the ultimate in being in the center of God's will.

Consequences of Being Out of God's Will

Once a tourist group was being shown an area of South Georgia. Looking up into a stand of oak trees, the guide said, "Yonder in the top of those oaks is the laziest man in Georgia!"

One member of the group, wishing to be sympathetic, replied, "Sitting in a tree on a hot day is no crime, is it?"

The guide replied, "Yes, but that man laid down on an acorn forty years ago!"

Being in the wrong place can bring tragic consequences. I want to name two consequences of being out of God's will.

Wasted Time

When you are not in God's will, you waste precious time which you were given by God to fulfill your purpose in life. "To every thing there is a season, and a time to every purpose under the heaven" (Eccl. 3:1). Time is a gift from God. Paul said at Mars Hill: "For in him we live, and move, and have our being" (Acts 17:28). If we are out of God, our living, moving, and being are wasted.

A man started taking violin lessons from an expert teacher. For several years he studied and practiced, becoming a very good musician. One day he asked his teacher if he would ever become a great violinist. "No," the teacher answered.

The man was shocked! He asked, "Do I not have the abilities? Do I not practice diligently? Do I not have the desire?"

The wise teacher said, "Yes. You have the abilities, desire, and work habits. Your problem is, you waited too late to begin!"

Moses is a classic example of losing precious time. True, Moses accomplished great things from age 80 to 120. How wonderful if God could have used him from age forty to eighty, instead of having him on the back side of the desert learning about himself and God. I have talked to many preachers who lost precious time, because they did not answer God's first call.

What if Mary had not taken advantage of the only time she had to anoint the feet of Jesus? (John 12:1-8). Mary felt led of God to anoint Jesus at that particular time, and, if she had not been faithful, Jesus never would have been anointed for His burial (John 12:7). When we are in God's will, we take advantage of the time allotted to us.

Wasted Resources

Not only is our time tragically wasted when out of God's will, but also our resources. The law of atrophy is use it or lose it. The writer of Ecclesiastes urges all youth to know God while they are young and in command of all their physical resources. Solomon says: "Remember now thy Creator in the days of thy youth, while the evil days come not, nor the years draw nigh, when thou shalt say, I have no pleasure in them" (Eccl. 12:1). Then, the preacher talks about how the physical resources begin to fade: the hands (keepers of the house), shoulders (strong men), teeth (grinders), eyes (those that look out of windows), ears (sound of the grinding is low), and voice (daughters of music brought low). Other characteristics are given: insomnia, fear of heights, white hair, weakness in lungs, spinal column, and heart. We must know and serve God when He calls us. It's best to start as a child.

When I think of wasted resources, I cannot help but remember Samson. All that strength, power, and purpose going to waste in a pagan prison! Out of God's will.

I believe one of the most tragic experiences we've ever had at our church took place one morning when a seventy-year-old man accepted Christ. He had been ill for a long time. His brother had shared Christ with him, and God was invited into his life. He stood before us that morning, weak and emaciated, and we felt so sorry for him. He insisted upon being baptized that morning. We normally wait at least a week so the candidate can study about baptism and be counseled. But, this man insisted on being baptized that morning. Our associate pastor took him and baptized him in front of all the congregation at the close of the service. This was certainly the time for this man, because he died the following Thursday.

I have often thought of the tragic waste in this true story. Seventy years of life without anything to show for Christ! He lived four days as a saved person. Our resources are not utilized when we are out of God's will.

The Cure

"What should I do when I do not know God's will?" Let us begin by examining a tremendous event in the life of Paul. We have before us in Acts 16:6-10 a turning point in history. The gospel is about to go to Europe and the Western world. The fate and eternal destiny of several continents will be in one little boat.

Remember Paul's second missionary journey. He and Barnabas separated in chapter 15, and now Paul travels with Silas and Timothy. The team started east, seeing lost souls every where. But, God blocked this direction (v. 6). They could not go to Asia; they turned northward and headed to Bithynia. However, "the Spirit suffered them not" (v. 7). A pastor was seen nervously pacing his office floor. "I'm in a hurry but God's not!" God wasn't ready for these two harvest-filled places yet.

Paul finally ran out of land as he came westward to Troas. That night Paul had his famous "Macedonian Vision" as God revealed His will to him. As a result of following God's perfect will, look where the gospel went: Philippi, Thessalonica, Berea, Athens, Corinth, and even Rome.

The key for us in this passage concerning God's will which lies in a phrase, in verse 10: "And after he had seen the vision, immediately we endeavored to go into Macedonia, *assuredly gathering* that the Lord had called us for to preach the gospel unto them" (author's italics). The phrase "assuredly gathering" is one word in the Greek: *sumbibazo. Sumbibazo* means to prove, to conclude, or to knit together.

It would help tremendously for us to see how this word *sumbibazo* is used in another passage. After Paul was saved, we read that he "increased the more in strength, and confounded the Jews which dwelt at Damascus, *proving* that this is very Christ" (Acts 9:22, author's italics). The word *proving* is the same as the phrase "assuredly gathering," *sumbibazo*. In other words, to prove that Jesus is the Christ or Messiah, Paul literally knit together the evidence from the Old Testament for these people. The following is how I believe he would *sumbibazo* that Jesus is Christ:

- Messiah would be of the tribe of Judah (Gen. 49:10).
- Messiah would be from David's line (2 Sam. 7:11-16).
- Messiah would be born in Bethlehem (Mic. 5:2).
- Messiah would be born of a virgin (Isa. 7:14).
- Messiah would die for our sins (Isa. 53:4-6).
- Messiah would die by crucifixion (Ps. 22:6)
- Messiah would be raised from the dead (Ps.16:10).

"Putting all these together" would form a picture of who the Messiah would be: Paul says the Person is Jesus of Nazareth. Jesus fulfilled all the parts of the Messiah puzzle.

In determining God's will, Paul "assuredly gathered" from all the evidence that God wanted him to go into Macedonia. We learn, then, that finding God's will is like *putting a puzzle together.* Different parts come together to convince or prove to us the way to go.

There are four parts to the "guidance puzzle" that we will mention in answering the question: "What should I do when I don't know God's will?"

God's Word

If I had to ask you one question to determine your "spiritual I.Q.," it would be: How much time do you spend in God's Word? The first important way in which God reveals His will is through His Word. His Word is a "lamp unto my feet, and a light unto my path" (Ps. 119:105). Do you really know how to read the Bible?

The positive commands are to be obeyed and the negative commands are to be heeded. When you abide in Him and His words abide in you, you can ask what you will, and it will be done unto you (John 15:7). Ask God to show you His Word concerning a subject or need. Examine that subject in your concordance. See what the Word says about it. God will give you a positive or negative command about it.

Many times "the word is nigh thee, even in thy mouth, and in thy heart" (Rom. 10:8). Sometimes people make a hard thing out of God's will, and His Word has already spoken clearly and conclusively about it. For instance, if you love someone and he or she is an unbeliever and you're wanting to know God's will, no need agonizing! Read 2 Corinthians 6:14; the answer is clear. If your job offer does not honor God, no need agonizing! Read 1 Corinthians 10:31; the answer is clear. The first step in finding God's will is to search the Scriptures (Matt. 22:29).

Circumstances

This is how it happened with Paul: God kept closing doors through circumstances. Soon Paul could not go any way but west toward Macedonia. Look for God's hand in circumstances. "For promotion cometh neither from the east, nor from the west, nor from the south. But God is the judge: he putteth down one, and setteth up another" (Ps. 75:6-7).

There was once a woman who felt God was calling her to be a missionary. Before she could be accepted, her sister died, leaving this woman as the only one to care for her sister's four children. She could not go to the mission field because of the urgent need of the children. So she stayed home and reared the children. Each was saved and all four became missionaries! Instead of God getting one missionary, He got four. God can speak to you through circumstances.

One of my favorite stories is that of Ida Scudder who came from a great history of missionaries. She came to America to go to school, vowing that there was one thing she'd never do: be a medical missionary. However, she rushed home to be with a critically-ill mother, and God spoke to her heart one evening. Three times that night men came to the door needing a female doctor to help their wives. Those women died, and Ida Scudder saw through these circumstances the will of God for her life.

God used the tragic circumstances in Joseph's life to save an entire nation. We know that "all things work together for good to them that love God, to them who are the called according to his purpose" (Rom. 8:28). Be alert! God may be speaking to you through happenings in your life. See which way the spiritual wind is blowing.

Inner Convictions

One of my wife's favorite verses is Colossians 3:15, "And let the peace of God rule in your hearts." Is there a peace about your decision? The word, *rule*, literally means for the Holy Spirit to be the Umpire or Referee. I believe there will be an inside voice Who will guide you. "And thine ears shall hear a word behind thee, saying, This is the way, walk ye in it, when ye turn to the right hand, and when ye turn to the left" (Isa. 30:21). Isn't that a profound verse! The Bible is saying that there will be inner drawings on our hearts as we seek to find God's will. Is God speaking to you about something?

Let me mention two characteristics of the inner convictions which will speak to you. First, God's voice within you will be *captivating.* You will know that something different is happening in you! The person, the event, the need, the Scripture, the thought—whatever God is using to speak to you—will be captivating. Paul was impressed someway not to go to Asia and Bithynia. The inner voice will be captivating. Secondly, the inner voice will be *constant.* In other words, the call will not be spasmodic or erratic. You won't be able to get God's voice off your mind for very long. William Carey, one of the fathers of the modern missions movement, would read his Bible, read books by Captain Cook, and pray over his homemade map of the world. Should he leave his country and business to go into missions? The inner convictions were captivating and constant. God spoke to him through Isaiah 54:2-3 with a call so captivating and constant that he went to India.

Counselors

Another way God makes known His will is through spiritual friends. Two are better than one (Eccl. 4:9-12). "Where no counsel is, the people fail: but in the multitude of counselors, there is safety" (Prov. 11:14). Have you noticed that this principle is practiced in sports? The basketball coach calls for a time-out and confers with several assistants briefly before announcing the next strategy of the game. A quarterback calls time-out and goes to the sidelines to discuss the crucial play with the head coach and assistants. Counselors are utilized in practically every area of life.

Do you have spiritual friends with whom you can talk and pray about God's will? These friends should be spiritual people—grounded in the Word of God. They should be confidential people: "Confidence in an unfaithful man in time of trouble is like a broken tooth, and a foot out of joint" (Prov. 25:19).

God was speaking to young Samuel, but Samuel did not know how to recognize the voice of God (1 Sam. 3:7). The child agonized when God spoke to him and was so confused that he mistook God's voice for another person's voice. How fortunate Samuel was that the experienced priest, Eli, realized what was happening. He instructed Samuel in how to answer God: "if he call thee, that thou shalt say, Speak, Lord; for thy servant heareth" (1 Sam. 3:9). The next time God spoke, Samuel was prepared and answered his call. Do you have someone as a spiritual friend or counselor who can help you determine the will of God?

In closing, I believe that, outside of my personal decision to accept Christ, the call to the ministry was the most important need in my life in finding God's will. I was a senior in high school when I was saved. As graduation neared, thoughts about the future and my place in life dominated my waking moments. Upon salvation, I had a tremendous desire to study the Bible and share with other people. That summer I went to Music Week at Ridgecrest Conference Center in North Carolina with our youth choir. One night I heard a musical where the crucifixion of Christ was vividly portrayed on stage. I was moved by the musical and requested permission to walk back to the cabin. I felt the impulse to go through the woods. I came to an old foundation of a house with the steps still joined to it. I sat down on those steps, began to weep and pray, and heard God say: "Preach the word; be instant in season, out of season" (2 Tim. 4:2). This is number one—the *Word of God.* I had memorized this verse and it went through my mind over and over. All that night and throughout the week, I kept hearing that verse and thinking: "Is God calling me to preach? These feelings were captivating and constant.

Upon returning to Florida, there was an invitation waiting for me to preach. A minister in my hometown had the mumps and could not go to his country church. How did he know God was dealing with me in North Carolina? Over the next month, I talked to pastors, deacons, and trusted friends. Much advice was given to me. One word I shall never forget came from an older preacher who said: "Son, if you can do anything but preach, do it. That means you aren't called!" I've thought about that many times. I cannot see myself ever doing anything but pastoring God's people and preaching God's Word.

When you are struggling to determine God's will for your life, search the *Scriptures*, prayerfully and carefully. Listen for God's message through *inner convictions*—this message will be captivating and constant. Share your burden with *counselors* who are spiritual, confidential, and honest. Be aware of what God is doing in and around your life through *circumstances.* May all of us come to the point where we may say: "I delight to do thy will, O my God" (Ps. 40:8).